POTTER CRAFT

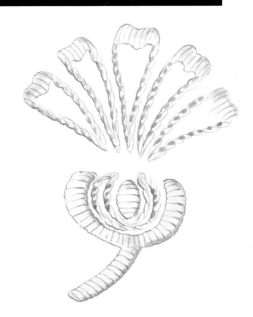

embroidery

POTTER CRAFT

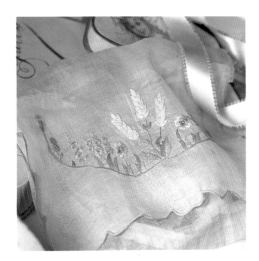

embroidery

techniques • projects • patterns • motifs

Karen Elder

Photography by Pia Tryde

POTTER
CRAFT

New York

Text, design, and layout copyright © 1995 Quadrille Publishing Limited
Project photography copyright © 1995 Pia Tryde
Detail photography copyright © 1995 Peter Cassidy, Dave King

Published in the United States by Potter Craft,
an imprint of the Crown Publishing Group,
a division of Random House, Inc., New York.
www.crownpublishing.com
www.clarksonpotter.com

POTTER CRAFT and CLARKSON N. POTTER are trademarks and POTTER and colophon are
registered trademarks of Random House, Inc.

Originally published in Great Britain by Quadrille Publishing Limited, London, and in the United
States by Clarkson Potter / Publishers, an imprint of the Crown Publishing Group, a division of
Random House, Inc., in 1995.

Library of Congress Cataloging-in-Publication Data is available.

ISBN–10: 0-307-33965-3
ISBN–13: 978-0-307-33965-2

Printed in China
Cover design by Laura Palese

10 9 8 7 6 5 4 3 2 1

First Potter Craft Edition

contents

Introduction

The joy of embroidery – the embellishment of fabric with stitching – lies not only in the finished work but also in the pleasurable hours involved in the execution of even the smallest piece. The dictionary describes embroidery as "inessential ornament" – a brutal description, for without embroidery the world would be a poorer place. Before the widespread availability of printed cloth and sophisticated weaves, the only means to decorate textiles was often embroidery. The dictionary is not so dismissive of painting, for the entry reads "representing or depicting by colors on a surface," but this could equally well apply to embroidery, for stitches are like the strokes of a pencil, pen, or brush in drawing and painting, and the variations on a theme just as limitless.

Perhaps embroidery's most exciting quality is its ability to fit any shape, almost without compromise. Next comes the notion that every embroiderer is making something unique and that no two pieces of work will ever be the same – invaluable in this age of mass production.

Much beautiful embroidery is even, fine, counted, and "perfect." However, the approach taken in this book is to free the mind and fingers to explore the possibilities of stitches, color, texture, and personal expression, rather than to focus on stitch perfection – evenness of stitches improves with practice.

The term "embroidery" encompasses many types of decoration of textiles, usually using a needle and some form of thread, bead, or sequin. For this book, the more specialized forms, such as canvaswork, goldwork, and counted thread work (except one piece of counted cross stitch) have been omitted in favor of providing a general grounding in free-form embroidery. The fifteen relatively straightforward projects use a simple repertoire of stitches that is easily accessible to anyone wishing to learn. Once these stitches have been mastered, it is possible to move on to more ambitious projects without difficulty; in the meantime, this approach demonstrates that fancy, precise, and highly skilled work is not always necessary to produce an effective, pretty, or impressive piece of work In fact, many of the designs in this book use only one or two stitches.

It is often thought that large doses of patience and skill are necessary to be a successful embroiderer, but it can be argued that patience is only needed for tedious work, which hardly applies to most embroidery. With a few easily learned stitches, much pleasure can be drawn from the process as well as from the finished piece.

Before you start

The vast array of fabrics, threads, needles, scissors, embroidery frames, and accessories available may appear daunting to the novice. Most of these materials and tools are designed with specific purposes in mind, so follow the guidelines provided in this chapter, and also take the advice of your needlework store to select the right materials for the projects you wish to make.

However, it is possible to use a huge variety of fabrics and threads that are not specifically designed for embroidery. Once you have explored techniques a little, and acquired some knowledge of how the various materials behave, you will be well equipped to choose the right weight of fabric for the thread, and a needle that will do a good job.

It is also interesting to look at traditional embroidery from different parts of the world, where local materials may be all that are available: roughly woven, brightly colored fabrics form the background of many

ethnic designs. Embroidery is integral to the lives of many less technically advanced communities, as it is the only way they have of adorning their clothes. There is a lot we can learn from their uninhibited approach.

materials & equipment

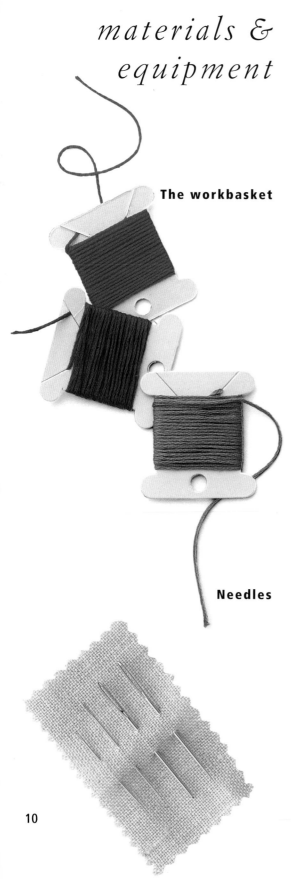

Embroiderers are fortunate in that no expensive or space-taking materials or equipment are necessary for the enjoyment and successful execution of a piece of stitching, or "work" as the ladies of leisure of past centuries were so fond of calling it. The added bonus is that fabric, threads, needles, and scissors are easy and light to carry with you, making embroidery an ideal pastime for traveling and vacations.

What is most important is that the materials and equipment selected for a project are of good quality and are appropriate for the task. With the right items in your workbasket, you will achieve a professional-looking result and have the satisfaction of knowing that your finished piece will give you pleasure for many years.

The workbasket

An embroidery workbasket need contain only a few tools for successful stitching. The essential items are:
• Embroidery scissors (see opposite), sewing scissors for cutting out fabric, and paper-cutting scissors.
• Tape measure.
• Dressmaker's pins and pincushion.
• Water-soluble marking pen and/or soft lead pencil for marking details.
• Transfer pencil and tracing paper, or dressmaker's carbon paper, if you are going to transfer designs yourself.
• Tailor's chalk, for removable marking when sewing together projects.
• Assortment of needles (see below), thimble, and needlecase. Pincushions do not work well for needles, as they can disappear inside.

A few other tools can assist in achieving a good result:
• A few hoop frames (see opposite) in different sizes. Even if you prefer to work without a frame, there are times when it is a necessity – for example, when working large areas of satin stitch and other long stitches. French knots, too, are difficult to work without a frame. The work can be mounted onto a hoop in seconds.
• Thread bobbins. These are also extremely practical, for however carefully embroidery skeins are used, they can easily get tangled as the threads are withdrawn. Winding the thread onto a cardboard bobbin can save time and energy, and avoid frustration. Write the color number on the card for future reference.
• Magnifying glass that can hang around your neck. This will keep your hands free and is helpful not only for those with less-than-perfect eyesight, but also for working very small stitches, like the ones used in the Embroidered Buttons on page 88.

Needles

The starting point for successful embroidery is a good needle that is the right size and sharpness for the job in hand. It should also be shiny: the plating on needles gets scratched in time, so as soon as your needle feels sticky and appears slightly tarnished, it is time to change to a new one.
• The eye of the needle should be large enough to take the thread without difficulty, and the doubled thread should pass through the fabric with ease. If the thread does not do this, try a larger needle size.
• Very fine needles are often specified as

they run through fabric with ease, but for those with less nimble fingers they can be difficult to hold. Often a slightly larger one may be substituted successfully.
• Needle sizes are denoted by numbers: the lower the number, the larger the needle, so a size 1 needle is larger than a size 2, and so on.

Needles are often sold in packs of mixed sizes, allowing for some experimentation. The four types of needles used for embroidery are discussed opposite, but ultimately the choice is yours.

Crewel (embroidery) needles come in sizes 1 to 10. They have sharp points to pierce the fabric easily, and long eyes to take one or more strands of floss or fine wool threads. These are the needles used for most embroidery projects. Apart from the long eye, they are the same in length and point as ordinary sewing needles (sharps).

Tapestry needles come in sizes 13 to 26. They have rounded, blunt ends which slip between the warp and weft of fabrics such as blockweave and heavy evenweaves for counted thread embroidery (see page 15) without splitting them. They are ideal for use on needlepoint canvas, where a sharp point would catch. The oval-shaped eyes are generous in size to allow thick yarns to be threaded.

Chenille needles are identical to tapestry needles except for their sharp point. They are used for fabrics like twill and for thicker yarns that may not thread into a crewel (embroidery) needle.

Betweens (quilting needles) come in sizes 1 to 12. They are sharp ended and short, for quick, even stitching such as running stitch, backstitch, and stem stitch. They are also good for French knots, being easy to manipulate.

Scissors

A pair of small, really sharp, pointed scissors is an essential tool for every embroiderer. The blades should be sharp all the way along, especially at the point. A larger pair of scissors for cutting fabric is also necessary.

Embroidery frames

Hoops

For most kinds of embroidery a round tambour frame, or embroidery hoop frame, is a simple, cheap but useful tool. It consists of two wooden hoops that fit inside one another; the fabric is stretched over the smaller hoop and then the larger one is fitted over the top and a screw on the larger hoop is used to adjust the tension. A hoop helps keep the fabric smooth and the stitches flat, especially where long stitches, such as satin stitch, need to be made.
• If the area of embroidery is not too large, use a hoop into which the whole design will fit. On larger pieces, the hoop can be moved around.
• Always remove the hoop when you have finished working, as it can stretch and mark the fabric if left on between stitching sessions.
• A hoop holds the work much more evenly if the smaller hoop is bound with cloth. Wrap strips of cotton fabric or fabric tape all around the edge and work a few stitches to hold it in place.

The embroidery fabric will then sit more comfortably in the frame.
• There are also hoops that can be screwed to a table, or with a stand that you can sit on, leaving both hands free to work. The right hand is kept under the hoop and the left hand on top (vice versa for left-handed stitchers); with a little practice, this is a quicker way to work. The range of holders and stands for hoops and frames is too vast to explore in detail here, but the most important feature of any type of stand is that it holds the work firmly and does not wobble when in use.

Rectangular frames

If you like to work with a frame, large pieces of embroidery are best mounted onto a rectangular frame. Machine stitch a piece of fabric tape or a sturdy fabric strip around the edge of the fabric to be worked on, and then lace or stitch this onto the frame, depending on its design. This will take the main stress points away from the embroidery fabric, preventing distortion.

Thread

Just about any yarn or thread may be used for embroidery, providing it can be threaded through a needle and a suitable fabric found for it – even soft string might embroider well on very coarse fabric. However, until you have used a few different types of thread it is better to stick to threads designed for embroidery which are tried and tested for strength and colorfastness. It would be a pity to spend many hours plying your needle, only to find that the thread was not strong enough for the job or that the colors ran when washed or dampened for pressing (see page 20).

Embroidery threads are packaged in many different types of skein and hank. Some are wound so that lengths can be pulled out easily, as in cotton floss. However, many require that the skein bands be removed and the yarn untwisted or unfolded before they can be used. These types, for example pearl cotton and *coton à broder* (see page 14), often fall out into a skein that can be cut at each end to create a group of threads the right length for stitching. If you knot the group loosely in the center, it will stay neat. Do not use elastic bands to hold strands together as they damage the thread.

A stitch can take on a very different appearance when worked in different threads. Try out a variety of thicknesses of thread in one stitch to see the effects. Some are much easier to execute in finer yarns, but the boldness of thick corded threads can create a dramatic impact.

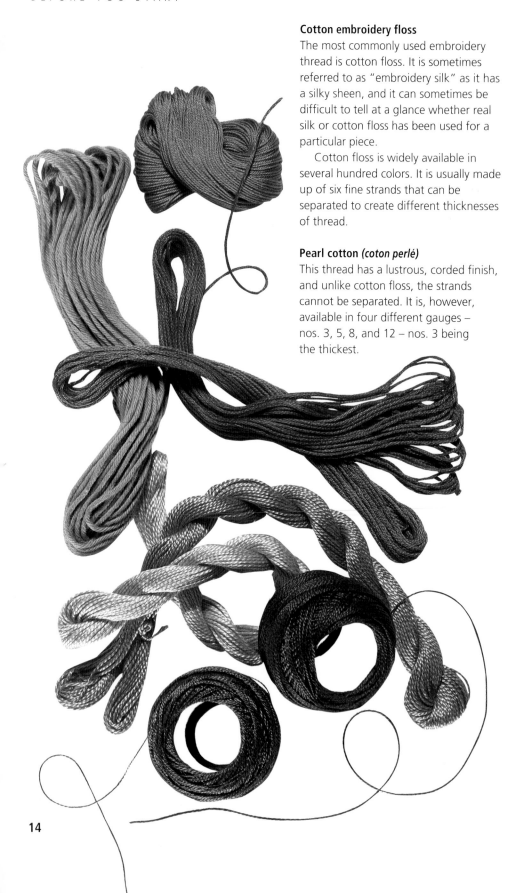

Cotton embroidery floss

The most commonly used embroidery thread is cotton floss. It is sometimes referred to as "embroidery silk" as it has a silky sheen, and it can sometimes be difficult to tell at a glance whether real silk or cotton floss has been used for a particular piece.

Cotton floss is widely available in several hundred colors. It is usually made up of six fine strands that can be separated to create different thicknesses of thread.

Pearl cotton (coton perlé)

This thread has a lustrous, corded finish, and unlike cotton floss, the strands cannot be separated. It is, however, available in four different gauges – nos. 3, 5, 8, and 12 – nos. 3 being the thickest.

Silk embroidery floss

Silk embroidery floss is similar to cotton floss in its thickness and composition, and can be used for the same purposes.

Coton à broder (broder spécial)

This is a single-thread mercerized cotton thread with a slight sheen. It is especially suitable for cutwork, where the strands of floss may not pull through evenly on close buttonhole stitching.

Soft embroidery cotton

This relatively thick, single-thread yarn has a matt finish. It is best used on loose-weave fabrics, as it is difficult to pull through tightly woven ones and can look lumpy unless a suitable stitch is chosen, such as French knots.

Flower thread

Flower thread is similar in appearance to coton à broder except that it has a matt finish as opposed to a sheen.

Crewel wool or Persian yarn

These are the wool threads most commonly used for surface embroidery. They are both fine threads that can be used either singly or stranded together, as required. Crewel wool comes as a single thread and Persian yarn comes with three threads together, which can be separated.

Knitting yarn

Some fine knitting yarns – for example, two-ply botany wool – can also be used for embroidery, but care should be taken to ensure that it is good quality, 100% wool, and colorfast.

Other threads

There are also metallic threads, random-dyed yarns, and numerous varieties of silk, cotton, and synthetic threads available. Once you have mastered the basic stitches, experimenting with these more unusual threads can bring individuality to your work.

Fabrics The main characteristic of specially produced embroidery fabrics is the evenness of the weave in both directions, where threads or blocks of threads per inch (2.5cm) are quoted in the fabric description. This is known as the "count." These fabrics are divided into two main groups:

• **Blockweave** fabrics have the warp and weft threads grouped to create a box-like structure, making it very easy to follow a cross stitch chart. Each stitch is worked over one block, or square, of the fabric. The finished size of the piece can thus be calculated with great accuracy. The most widely used blockweave fabric is Aida, which is available in a variety of weights, counts, and fibers to suit many uses. Most commonly used for cross stitch, Aida fabric is also suitable for most kinds of geometric patterning.

• **Evenweave** fabrics have, as the name suggests, the same number of warp and weft threads per square inch (centimeter). When working cross stitch on evenweaves, the crosses are usually made over two threads in each direction; for other stitches in counted thread work, the number of threads over which each stitch must be worked is usually indicated in the pattern. The finished size of a design can then be calculated fairly easily when working from a chart on a specified count of fabric. Evenweaves are the best fabrics for pulled thread work and drawn thread work, and also for Hardanger work – a counted satin stitch cutwork technique – all of which are unsuitable for blockweave fabrics.

Choosing fabrics

All these embroidery fabrics are available in good needlework shops. However, the choice need not be restricted to these; many other good-quality fabrics are suitable for embroidery, and this is demonstrated in the projects in this book. The choice of fabric is dependent on the type of embroidery, the chosen yarn, and the use to which the finished item will be put. These factors will determine the looseness of the weave, the degree of texture in relation to the thread, and the durability and washability of the fabric. As a general rule, heavy threads and yarns are unsuitable for very fine fabrics, and fine threads may be lost on a heavy or textured cloth.

preparation

Time taken in preparing a piece of fabric for embroidery is time well spent. Placing the design with care, transferring the pattern using the most suitable method, and ensuring that you have the right equipment can save trouble in the long run. It is also worth experimenting with pattern markers to ensure that the pattern transfers clearly to the chosen fabric, and that it will wash out properly if required. Always press your fabric before starting, so that you have a smooth, flat surface on which to work.

Preparing fabric

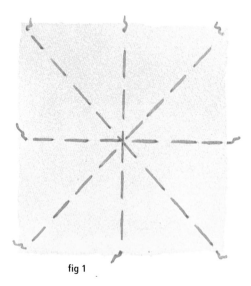

fig 1

The first step when embarking on a new piece of embroidery is to plan the placement of the design.

• Finding and marking the center of the fabric is necessary for both geometric and free-form patterns. To do this, fold the fabric in half and baste along the crease lines. Open; then fold the fabric the other way and baste along the intersecting crease, so that the fabric is divided into four equal rectangles.

• To mark the corner positions for rectangles, make two more folds in the fabric, this time diagonally, and baste along the crease lines as before (fig 1).

Within this framework it is simple to lay out symmetrical and formal patterns, while free-form designs and motifs are easier to place if these axes are marked.

• Work overcast stitches along the edges of the fabric or cover them with masking tape before starting to stitch to prevent loose, frayed threads catching in the work. However, only use masking tape if you are going to trim off the edge later. The glue will mark the fabric.

• Once the design has been chosen, it may be necessary to enlarge or reduce it in size to fit the project for which it is intended. This is now a simple process, if carried out on a photocopier – the photocopier operator will be able to do the calculations for you to make your chosen design a specific size.

Transferring patterns

To transfer the design onto your fabric, you will need to use a method that is sympathetic to the work.

• For easily washed embroidery, tracing (method 1) is a good choice.

• If the fabric is too thick for the pattern to be traceable through it, dressmaker's carbon paper (method 2) is a good alternative, as the marks will wash out.

• If the embroidery will cover the markings completely, then making an iron-on transfer (method 3) creates the clearest image.

Whichever method you choose, be sure to transfer the whole pattern before starting to stitch, for once stitching has begun it is difficult to lay the fabric flat. In addition, the placement of free-form designs will become difficult to judge and symmetrical designs will become distorted and may not join up successfully if marked out piecemeal.

Method 1: tracing

The simplest and often most successful method on thin fabrics is to trace the pattern on directly, using a water-soluble pen or very fine pencil. The problem with the latter is that the lead can smudge and make the embroidery thread dirty. However, any dirt should wash out, except on very pale colors. Water-soluble pen markings can fade away before the embroidery is finished, but are fine for small projects.

1 Draw or trace the design onto a piece of tracing paper or thin white paper and tape it to a window.

2 Tape the fabric on top and trace the pattern onto it.

Method 2: dressmaker's carbon paper

This special fabric carbon comes in different colors, so choose one that will be clearly visible on your fabric. The drawback is that the markings may brush off before the embroidery is finished. Pressing will prevent this, but the markings will then be permanent.

1 Draw, trace, or photocopy the pattern you wish to transfer.

2 Place the fabric on a clean, flat surface and tape it down using masking tape.

3 Place the carbon paper face down on the fabric and tape to secure.

4 Place the pattern on top and tape it down. Using a ballpoint pen, trace carefully over the pattern.

5 Turn up one corner to see if the design has transferred successfully before removing the paper. Try not to lean on the carbon paper with your hand as it may smudge onto the fabric.

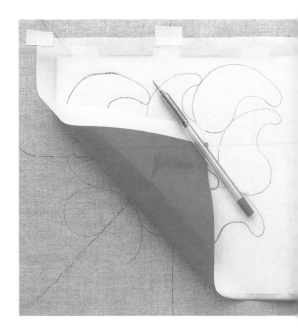

Method 3: making a transfer

Special transfer pencils are available for transferring embroidery patterns, but on many fabrics they do not work well. Synthetic fabrics and those with a finish or dressing work best, but the problem can be overcome by giving other fabrics a thorough spraying with spray starch just before transferring the pattern. Test the transfer pencil on a small piece of the fabric before using. Transfer pencil may not wash out, so it is only suitable where the embroidery covers the marking fully.

1 Trace the design onto a sheet of thin tracing paper.

2 Turn the tracing over and trace the back using the transfer pencil.

3 Press the fabric that you wish to use, spray well with starch if it has no dressing on it, and then pin the transfer in place (transfer-pencil side down). Press slowly using a hot iron (do not use a steam setting).

4 Turn up one corner to see if the design has transferred successfully before unpinning the paper.

from start to finish

Threading the needle, positioning the first stitch, and starting and finishing threads – the beginning and end of any piece of work, as well as the many threads in between – is rarely explained, but it is of fundamental importance. Making the first stitch, happy in the knowledge that it is correctly and firmly placed, as well as neatly done, gives much-needed confidence when embarking on a new piece of embroidery.

Threading needles

Threading a needle is something that many people find difficult due either to poor eyesight or because they don't know the best way to do it. A good way to thread a needle is as follows:
1 Hold the needle in your right hand (left if you are left-handed), and with your other hand, loop the thread over the point of the needle and pull it tight.
2 Holding this loop firmly between your thumb and index finger, turn the needle around, place the eye over the loop and push it down so that the thread passes through it.

Where to start

Where to start stitching a project is a fundamental question.
• It is always a good idea to work in a continuous flow, rather than starting in several different places and then finding that the work does not join up successfully.
• Where a design requires very dense stitching, it is easiest to start in the center with the main features and work outward, as for the Floral Tea Cozy project on page 60.
• For most patterns, but especially for geometric or symmetrical ones, be sure to draw the whole pattern before starting to stitch (see page 16).

Starting a thread

Your thread should be no longer than 20" (50cm). Not only are longer threads uncomfortable for the arm and shoulder, but they can also knot, twist, and fray.
• For most embroidery, the neatest way to start is to make a few small stitches, leaving the end of the thread at the front, within the "flight path" of your stitching – the space on the fabric that you intend to cover with the thread presently on your needle. It is important to cover the starting stitches within this section of embroidery to ensure that colors do not overlap, causing the thread of one piece of work to be inadequately masked by another color.
• Where small starting stitches would not be covered by the embroidery, for instance when working French knots or any exposed stitches, run the thread under a few stitches on the back before starting. Try not to run dark threads into light ones and vice versa, for they may show through. If you are starting where there are no stitches, leave a long thread at the back, then stitch it in when you have worked some embroidery.

Finishing a thread

This can be done in the same two ways as starting a thread.
• If you are continuing in the same color, make a couple of tiny stitches where they will be covered by the next thread. Leave the end on the top of the work, snipping it off when you reach it.
• If you are using a contrasting color, turn the work over and run the thread under a few stitches on the back. Never carry threads on the wrong side across an area that is not to be worked: not only can it spoil the tension, but it may show through when you have finished.
   It is important to cut thread ends off once they have been secured; thread ends left hanging will tangle and interfere with your stitching.

using this book

Stitches

For ease of reference, the stitches used in this book have been grouped into outline stitches, edging stitches, filling stitches, and embellishment stitches. Although the groupings describe the most usual application of each stitch, most are versatile enough to be used in any category. For example, herringbone stitch has been used as an edging stitch in the Red Outline Coverlet on page 27, and as an embellishment stitch to decorate the Crazy Patchwork on page 90; all linear stitches can be stitched in close rows to make them into filling stitches (see the Paisley Sampler pillow on page 44), while cross stitch could fit into any of the four categories.

Threads

The threads specified for the projects in this book are those that are most widely available. However, you can choose different threads, substitute silk for cotton, use fine pearl cotton in place of *coton à broder*, and make any changes that may suit your chosen fabric better than the thread specified. To achieve a similar effect to that illustrated, try to select a thread of the same weight. If a different effect is sought, a little experimentation will quickly give you an idea of how different fabrics and threads respond to the stitches used. Do not be afraid to try things out on a spare piece of fabric.

Quantities Every stitcher uses a different amount of thread. So much depends on how close together the stitches are worked, how much thread is used in starting and finishing, and also tension, that the quantities given for each project should be used as a guide only. As many of the pieces are old and the thread quantities therefore not tested, in these cases a close estimate is all that can be given.

Colors The dyeing of commercial embroidery threads is a sophisticated art and there should be no difference in the shade if extra thread is purchased at a later date. Wool thread is less reliable to color match, but some variation in shade may enhance rather than detract from the finished embroidery.

Finishing

Instructions have been given for making the embroideries into useful items, but as this is an embroidery, not a sewing, book it is assumed that the reader is familiar with basic sewing skills.

caring for embroidery

Do not be frightened to use your newly worked embroidery. If the ends of the embroidery threads have been secured well, then your finished piece should be quite durable and you will be able to enjoy it without fear. Many hours of work have gone into making it, so it would be a pity to put it away because it might get damaged. If the work is kept clean, and care is taken with cleaning, most embroidery should last a long time, especially if good-quality materials were used to start with.

Using old embroideries

If you have old pieces – pretty but not valuable – that you have inherited, collected, or worked in your childhood, you may be able to make good use of them in different ways from the original intention. On page 68, for example, a tablecloth has been turned into a pretty curtain which shows off the embroidery to better effect than as a tablecloth. Tray cloths can be joined together to make a larger "patchwork" piece for a bedspread or pillows, and where the fabric is stained or worn but the embroidery is still intact, pieces of the original can be appliquéd onto quilts, valances, or curtains.

Many old embroideries, especially those from the East, have faded over the years, which adds to their beauty. However, washing them could cause damage. They are best framed and hung on the wall out of direct sunlight.

Washing

Dust and strong sunlight are the main enemies of embroidery. However colorfast the threads are, strong sunlight will eventually bleach out some of the color, while dust will rot the fibers, especially wool. It is therefore important to keep embroidery clean.

With the exception of canvaswork; most cotton embroidery is washable. If the ends have been properly secured when starting and finishing (see page 18), and the colors are fast, some larger pieces may even be washed in a machine on a gentle cycle.

Due to environmental concerns, colorfastness is not always as strong as it has been in the past. It is best to wash colorfast cotton thread in plenty of hot water, because lukewarm or cold water increases the risk of color bleeding. Use a detergent recommended for delicates: avoid laundry detergents with chemicals added for color brightening and so on.

Do not put embroidery in the dryer; instead, roll up the wet piece of embroidery in a white towel and press very gently, before hanging it up to dry. Press the work while it is still slightly just damp, placing it face down on a thick towel to prevent the embroidery from flattening. The embroidery threads may not dry as quickly as the fabric, so lay it flat after pressing and leave until the threads are completely dry.

Never wash canvaswork embroidery (also known as needlepoint). Washing can shrink the needlepoint canvas, and it also removes the dressing that is added to keep the canvas in shape. In addition, the wool embroidery threads can become matted and fluffy, spoiling its appearance. A vigorous shaking should remove dust, but if the embroidery is really dirty, dry cleaning is recommended for best results.

Storing

The best way to store embroidery which will not be displayed for some time is to lay it flat in a drawer, wrapped in acid-free tissue paper. Do not use plastic bags, as the static attracts dust and the textiles will not be able to breathe. Make sure that the pieces are fully covered with tissue, otherwise any protruding edges will yellow, and then lay a clean folded sheet over the top.

Outline embroidery

Outline embroidery is probably one of the oldest forms of the craft, echoing the simplest form of drawing: much of the Bayeux tapestry is wrought in outline, and that is over 900 years old. The popularity of outline work in the mid-1880s was probably the result of patterns being sold which had already been outlined with stitching in one color. In the United States outline work really caught on, with motifs being published not only in the women's press but in art magazines as well. An American author wrote at the time: "As the chief beauty of outline work depends upon grace and fidelity of form, it is naturally a craft demanding poetic instinct as well as delicate manipulation." This is perhaps a distorted view, for the ease and quickness of its execution must have been a major factor in the popularity of the technique, and the mostly naïve quality of the motifs demands little in the way of "delicate manipulation."

The work was normally stitched with cotton embroidery floss in a single color, and for some reason – probably fashion – this was usually red. Thus the work became known as "redwork." Sayings were often incorporated into redwork designs, a common one being worked on pairs of pillowcases, one saying "I slept and dreamed that life was beauty," and the other "I woke to find that life was duty."

outline stitches

Outline stitches are the simplest embroidery stitches and outline work is the nearest that embroidery gets to line drawing, for it lends itself to the successful interpretation of simple subjects, even for the novice stitcher. The work is often undertaken in a single color, giving it a naïve charm in which the motif is more important than the stitching. More ambitious designs can also be executed in outline, using lines of embroidery to shade motifs and introducing a range of colors and textures using different shades and threads. Outline stitches can also be used to fill motifs with interesting texture by working lines of stitching as close together as required. Chain stitch is commonly used in this way, as is stem stitch (see the Paisley Sampler Pillow on page 44).

Running stitch

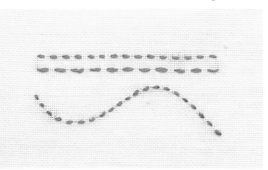

This is one of the most basic of all stitches for any kind of sewing and is used both for decoration and for strengthening. It consists of short stitches running in and out of the fabric in a single line. In embroidery, running stitches give a lightness to small curves, stalks of plants, and any other place where solid lines may be too heavy, the gaps suggesting to the eye that something is there when in fact it is not.

Working from right to left, the

fig 1

needle is taken in and out of the fabric to create a broken line of stitches of a size to suit the embroidery (fig 1).

Laced running stitch

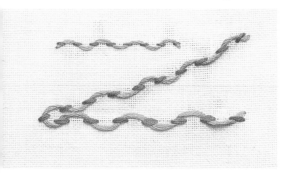

Running stitch can be embellished by lacing it with a contrasting color to form a decorative border, when it is called laced running stitch (fig 2). It is quick and easy to do and looks impressive. The lacing is done once the running stitch is complete, and does not pass through the background fabric. The use of a small, blunt-ended tapestry needle for the lacing enables the needle and thread to pass under rather than pierce the existing embroidery. In the Crazy

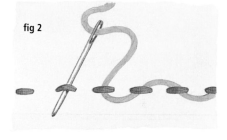

fig 2

Patchwork (see page 90), it has been used to decorate one of the seams between the patches.

Backstitch

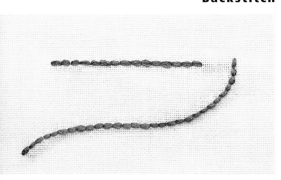

The line produced by backstitch is similar to running stitch, but is continuous, not broken. It is the best stitch for making long, straight lines, as in the Indian Valance (see page 64), but can also be used for curves, though it does not curve as smoothly as stem stitch (opposite). It is made by taking a long stitch forward underneath the fabric and a short backward stitch on top, joining with the previous stitch (fig 3).

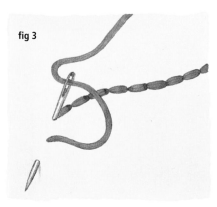

fig 3

Pekinese stitch

This decorative stitch is backstitch laced with looped thread (fig 4). Just as for laced running stitch (opposite), use a blunt-ended needle for the lacing. It is particularly important to keep an even and fairly loose tension for the best effect. More than one thread can be used for lacing, giving many possibilities for contrasts in color and texture in what is a very simple stitch.

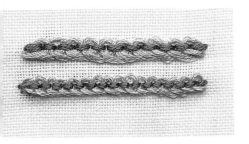

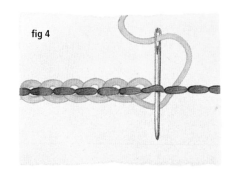

fig 4

Stem stitch

As its name suggests, stem stitch is used for plant stems, but also for outlines where an unbroken, smooth-running line is called for. The stitches overlap one another, and stitching at slightly different angles can give a thicker or thinner line. For a broad, twisted effect, the needle should pierce and emerge through the fabric on either side of the design line (fig 5). For narrow lines of stem stitch, work along the design line itself (fig 6).

1 Start by making a stitch as for running stitch, at the required angle.

2 Bring the needle up halfway back along the previous stitch. Repeat step 2 along the stitching line.

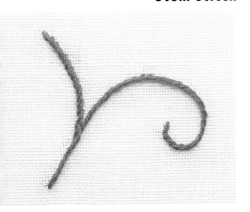

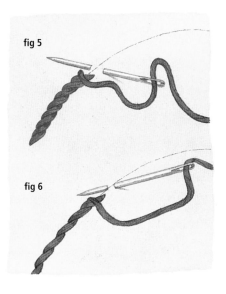

fig 5

fig 6

Chain stitch

Although chain stitch is a simple technique, it is very effective. Worked as an outline stitch it is quick and adaptable. Most Indian wool embroidery (crewel) is worked in chain stitch only, executed using a hook for speed. This is sometimes called "tambour" work, because the fabric is stretched tight across a hoop – like the surface of a tambourine. The sharply pointed tambour hook is punched through the fabric, picking up the thread from underneath. Early sewing machines worked in the same way, producing chain stitch instead of the familiar straight stitch of today.

There are several versions of chain stitch, but the simplest one is used for the crewelwork on the Crewelwork Pansies (see page 30), worked with an ordinary chenille needle.

1 Bring the thread up through the fabric. Holding the thread down with the left thumb, insert the needle where, or close to where, it emerged. Bring the point out a short distance away in the direction in which the stitches are to lie, looping the thread underneath (fig 7).

2 Pull the thread through and continue the chain in the same way (fig 8).

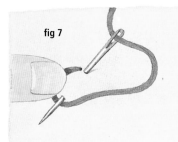

fig 7

fig 8

red outline coverlet

Stitches used
stem stitch (page 25),
French knots (page 76),
herringbone stitch (page 76).

This American embroidery is made up of ninety separate pieces each carrying its own, often rather unusual, motif. The simplicity and naïvity of the patterns are what make the coverlet so appealing, providing endless speculation as to why its creator chose to embroider a potato, a bucket, or a piece of cheese alongside the more usual subjects of flowers and animals. Eight of these motifs are illustrated below and overleaf. However, the joy of undertaking a piece like this lies in gathering together designs and symbols that relate to your own life, for it is the individuality of the work that is its most important attribute.

Sometimes these coverlets would be stitched by a number of people, but this appears to be the work of one person, for the stitching is close and regular. The date 1903 is embroidered in one of the squares. The coverlet would make a superb wall hanging (see page 23) and could also double as a tablecloth.

You will need
Medium-weight cotton fabric, to create
    as many squares as required – the
    pieces on this coverlet measure
    approximately 8″ (21cm) square when
    finished (seam allowance ¾″/2cm)
Crewel (embroidery) needle size 5 or 6
Cotton embroidery floss in the color
    of your choice

To work the embroidery
1 Draw your designs on separate squares of paper, using the motifs given here and overleaf, or creating some others of your own. Transfer onto the fabric by any of the methods described on pages 16–17.
2 Using all six strands of the floss throughout, embroider the squares separately. Work all the outlines in stem stitch and add details such as flower centers and animal eyes in French knots.

To finish
1 Lay the squares on a large table or on the floor and move them around until you are satisfied with the arrangement. Machine stitch the squares together into strips. Trim the seams to approximately ⅜″ (1cm) and press open.
2 Then sew the strips together, trimming the seams and pressing them open as before. It is important to baste first, so that the squares fit well and do not slip out of place when running through the sewing machine.
3 Sew over the seams with herringbone stitch, which will disguise the joins cleverly as well as securing the raw edges at the back of the coverlet.
On this piece, the outside edges have been turned under twice and secured by herringbone stitch, too, eliminating the need for normal hemming and providing a decorative border.

One of the whimsical images on the coverlet
is shown here actual size. More motifs to trace
and transfer are given overleaf.

A selection of the motifs used on the coverlet, shown actual size. Trace and transfer onto the fabric, adding other images of your choice.

crewelwork pansies

Stitches used
chain stitch (page 25),
stem stitch (page 25),
lazy daisy stitch (page 75).

Reputed to be the favorite flowers of Queen Elizabeth I, pansies are now in vogue once again. With their relatively uniform shape and idiosyncratic petal formation, they make particularly good subjects for simple outline embroidery. The flower colors, too, are distinctive, and their richness is enhanced by the depth of shades that are characteristic of wool embroidery yarns.

Crewelwork – sometimes called Jacobean work, from the embroidered hangings popular in England during the latter part of the seventeenth century – is embroidery executed in wool yarns. It is not clear whether the name comes from the wool yarn or from the art form itself, but the fine two-ply yarn that is used for this kind of embroidery is generally referred to as crewel wool.

Some of the stitchwork in traditional crewel embroidery is extremely ornate and requires a certain amount of skill and experience. However, it need not always be so, as quite simple stitches can be used in exactly the same way as embroidery with cotton or silk threads. These pansies are stitched in chain stitch – which can be used as an outline as well as a filling stitch – and a little stem stitch.

You will need
For the pillow:
20" (50cm) square backing fabric
14" (35cm) zipper
Matching sewing thread
18" (45cm) square pillow form
For the cord trimming (optional):
3 11yd (10m) skeins tapestry yarn (or wool sport-weight knitting yarn) in toning color (Prussian blue in the pillow illustrated)
Matching buttonhole thread, or doubled sewing thread
Hand drill with cup hook fixed to bit (optional)
Crewel (embroidery) needle size 2 or 3

For the embroidery:
20" (50cm) square fine evenweave linen twill fabric
Chenille needle size 22
Cardboard or stiff paper, 20" (50cm) square approx
Wool embroidery yarn in Appletons or Paternayan colors shown on page 33

To work the embroidery
1 Enlarge the pattern given on page 33 to 156% on a photocopier. Transfer the pattern onto the linen twill fabric using method 2 or method 3 described on pages 16–17.
2 Start by stitching the pansies, outlining the shapes with one or more rows of chain stitch in the colors shown in the key given with the pattern. The direction of the stitch is unimportant. Add the flowers on the mug in lazy daisy stitch with stem stitch stems.
3 When the flowers and mug are complete, make a cardboard cut-out "window" 13" (33cm) square. Place this over the embroidery and, when it is centered to your satisfaction, draw a line around the inside of the square using a pencil. This is the guideline for the embroidered border.
4 Work two rows of chain stitch along this line using the Prussian blue and airforce blue yarns. Add the crosses in chain stitch using pale aqua, starting at

This pansy motif, taken from the main design, shows the actual size of the flower.

fig 1

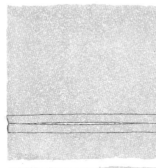

fig 2

fig 3

a corner and drawing them on freehand with a pencil as you go, with no attempt to make them uniform.

To finish

1 Cut the backing fabric into two across a line 6" (15cm) from the bottom.
2 Place the two pieces right sides together and lay the zipper along the center cut line. Mark where the zipper starts and finishes. Machine stitch up to this mark at each end (fig 1). Lay the fabric flat on an ironing board, face down, and press back the two short seams and the fold where the zipper is to be inserted (fig 2). Baste and machine stitch the zipper in place (fig 3).
3 Place the embroidery face downwards on a clean surface. Using a pencil, draw a square 2" (5cm) larger all around than the stitched border square (not the crosses) for the seam line.
4 With right sides together, machine stitch the front to the back along the pencil line around all four sides. Trim the seam allowance to ¾" (2cm) and snip across the corners. Turn the pillow cover right side and insert the pillow form.

To make and attach the cord

1 Divide each skein of tapestry yarn into three equal lengths, or cut three groups of three 3½yd (3.3m) lengths of knitting yarn. Knot together at each end.
2 Fix one end of one knotted length to a door frame or hook. Pull the yarn taut and wind it clockwise by hand or using the drill, until it starts to kink. Pin or weight down to keep it taut.
3 Repeat for the other two lengths, so they are the same length as the first.
4 Holding all three lengths taut in your hand, wind them together counter-clockwise, until you have a tight cord. It will not unravel.
5 Make a small cut about 1½" (4cm) long in the seam at the bottom of the pillow.
6 Starting at this opening, sew on the cord by hand. Make the stitches quite close together but do not pull them tight, as this will cause the edge of the pillow to pucker.
7 When the cord has been sewn on all around, push the cut ends through the 1½" (4cm) opening to the inside (fig 4), and stitch firmly to keep in place.

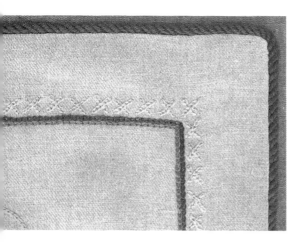

fig 4

	Appletons crewel wool	Paternayan Persian yarn			Appletons crewel wool	Paternayan Persian yarn
■ Wine red	148	900		▨ Pale aqua	521	506
▨ Lavender	102	313		▨ Pale olive	343	653
■ Purple	456	311		▨ Mid green	354	603
■ Indigo	106	571		■ Dark green	546	691
■ Purple blue	106	570		▨ Gold	473	726
■ Prussian blue	925	511		▨ Yellow	551	773
▨ Airforce blue	923	513		▨ Pale yellow	872	764
■ Juniper	157	520		☐ White	991	261

Quantity

One 27yd (25m) skein each of
Appletons crewel wool or one 8yd
(7.4m) skein each of Paternayan Persian
yarn is plenty to complete the design.
NB Paternayan Persian yarn is packaged
with three strands together, but only
one strand should be used throughout.

**Enlarge the pansy design to 156% on
a photocopier. Trace the outlines only
and transfer onto the fabric.**

Elegant edgings

Edging stitches make up one of the most important groups in embroidery, where the form follows the function to produce both practical and stunning results. For example, the closely worked buttonhole stitches that are intrinsic to cutwork not only create a firm edge which can be trimmed right up to the stitching, but accentuate the flow of the pattern in cutwork designs, or enhance the graceful effect of a scalloped edge while eliminating the need to hem the fabric.

Where a turned-up hem is required, drawn thread work is the classic method. It can be simple and elegant, or highly decorative and fancy, but its ability to secure a hem while creating decoration gives it an invaluable function. Pulled thread work can be used for hems in a similar way, but is more limited in its decorative possibilities.

Also included in this chapter are insertion stitches. These are used to

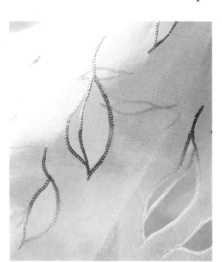

join two fabric edges together, replacing a conventional seam with a line of openwork embroidery. In this chapter the technique is shown on a pillowcase border, but it is also well suited to petticoats and nightgowns where seams would be cumbersome.

edging stitches

Stitches specially designed to finish, hem, or join pieces of fabric fall into three main groups. The first includes blanket stitch, which is generally used over fabric where the raw edge has been folded under. Buttonhole stitch – which resembles a closely worked blanket stitch – creates a firm enough edge without folding, from which the fabric can be cut away right up to the stitching if required. In the more open kinds of cutwork designs, buttonhole-stitch bars and double buttonhole-stitch bars provide extra strengthening and decoration.

The second group of edging stitches consists of drawn and pulled thread work, which create embellished border hems. The fabric threads above the hem are either removed, in the case of drawn thread work, or pulled tightly together in pulled thread work to form an attractive open finish. The third group of edging stitches comprises insertion stitches, used to join one fabric edge to another in a decorative and delicate manner.

Blanket stitch

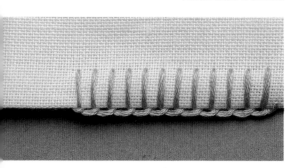

Worked over fabric where the raw edge has been folded under, blanket stitch provides a decorative and colorful finish to household items such as table linen and bed linen.

1 To start blanket stitch, the thread is brought up just above the edge of the fabric to anchor it firmly (fig 1).

2 From there on, the thread is taken down through the fabric and looped around the needle where it emerges clear of the edge (fig 2).

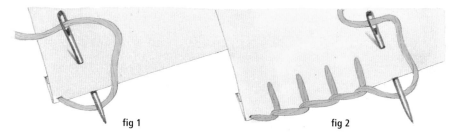

fig 1   fig 2

Buttonhole stitch

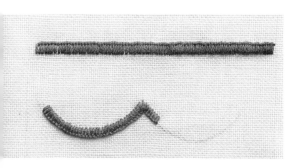

This stitch (fig 3) is worked in the same way as blanket stitch, but with the difference that in buttonhole stitch the stitches are close together to provide a firm edge that will not fray if the fabric is cut away.

It is used not only for buttonholes but is important for most forms of cutwork. This is a technique in which certain areas of the design are cut away right up to the looped edge of the buttonhole stitching to give an open, lacy appearance. A line of running stitches under the buttonhole stitch will help to strengthen the fabric in cutwork (fig 4).

Buttonhole can also be used as a filling stitch, worked in straight lines within a shape with the rows linked into one another by stitching into the looped edge of the row above. Alternatively, the stitches can follow the shape around in decreasing sizes until it is full.

fig 3

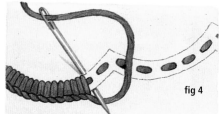

fig 4

Buttonhole-stitch bars

These decorative bars are used to hold large areas of cutwork in shape.

1 Single bars are created while working the running stitch foundation by taking a thread across a space and back again, three times, securing it with a small stitch each time (fig 5).

2 This bar is then covered in buttonhole stitch, with the stitches as close together as possible, without picking up the fabric underneath (fig 6).

3 The running stitch foundation is then continued around the design (fig 7).

4 When the running stitch foundation is complete, the design lines are covered with buttonhole stitch and the fabric is cut away where desired (fig 8), using a pair of small scissors with pointed tips.

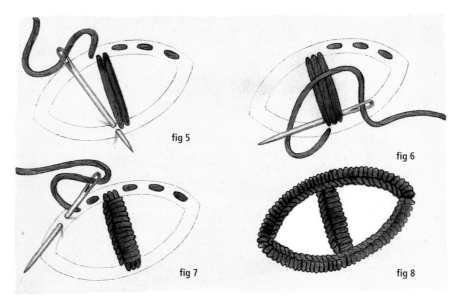

fig 5

fig 6

fig 7

fig 8

Double buttonhole-stitch bars

Where the buttonhole stitch in a cutwork design is to be cut away on both sides – for flower stems, for example – an intersecting stitch is required for strength. This is called double buttonhole stitch.

1 Work a row of running stitches as a bar over which the first row of buttonhole stitches will be worked, with the stitches spaced slightly apart.

2 Work a second row, stitching into the spaces left by the first row (fig 9).

3 Complete the outlining by working buttonhole stitching around the rest of the design.

4 Cut away the fabric where desired, leaving a strong, broad bar to hold two parts of the design together (fig 10).

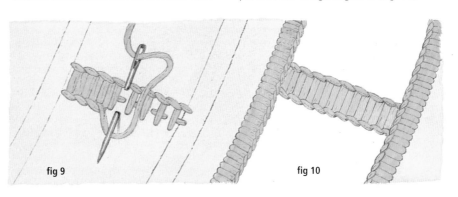

fig 9

fig 10

Drawn thread work

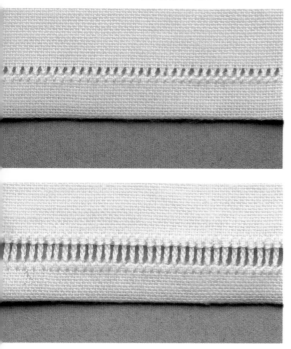

Drawn thread work describes needlework where some of the warp and weft threads have been pulled out of the fabric, leaving isolated threads which are then grouped and stitched over to create lines of little holes decorated with embroidery stitches. It can be extremely fancy or very simple and is useful for hemming a finished piece of embroidery. The most suitable fabrics for drawn thread work are evenweaves, from which threads can be cut and pulled out easily. The embroidery thread should match the weight of the fabric for the best effect.

Hemstitch

This is one of the simplest stitches used in drawn thread work and creates an attractive decorative hem. Note that the number of threads withdrawn and grouped will depend on the fabric count and the effect required.

1 To prepare fabric for hemstitching, mark or iron a line where the finished hem is to be, allowing enough extra fabric to make a turned-under hem.

2 Mark where the line of drawn thread work is to be and snip the threads at the center of the fabric. Gradually withdraw two to four threads inside the hemline, one thread at a time.

3 Turn under the hem and baste in place just below the isolated strands.

4 Start the embroidery from the right-hand side. The thread should emerge two fabric threads down from the loose, isolated threads. Care should be taken to ensure that the needle picks up the folded hem edge at the back when making each stitch.

5 Pass the needle behind four loose threads. Insert the needle behind the same four threads, bringing it out again two fabric threads down, as described above (fig 1). Repeat along the hem.

Ladder hemstitch

This variation is worked in the same way as hemstitch, with the tying stitches made along both edges of the drawn thread area (fig 2).

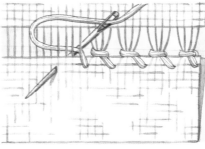

fig 1

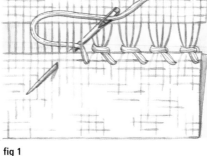

fig 2

Pulled thread work

Pulled thread work is embroidery where the fabric threads have been pulled by the stitches to create little holes, rather than being cut and withdrawn. The technique can create allover patterning using a variety of stitches, as well as simple edgings like the one produced by pin stitch, shown opposite. In embroidery books, pulled thread work is sometimes referred to as drawn fabric work, but for the purposes of clarity the two techniques on this page are better differentiated as described here.

An evenweave fabric such as linen, on which the threads can easily be counted, is the most suitable for pulled thread work. Use a fine tapestry needle for the stitching, as this has a blunt tip which will not split the fabric threads, and choose an embroidery thread of a comparable thickness to a thread taken from the fabric. For beautiful, regular-looking patterns, it is important to keep an even tension during stitching. An embroidery hoop will help to achieve this.

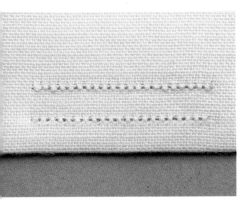

Pin stitch

This is a "pulled" rather than a "drawn" stitch, but is worked in a similar way to the drawn thread work stitches described on the previous page. Threads are grouped along the hemline to create a simple decoration, but no threads are withdrawn from the fabric.

Two or three threads are grouped together and stitched around twice, catching the hem underneath and creating a line of tiny holes (figs 3 and 4).

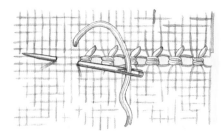

fig 3

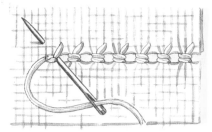

fig 4

Insertion stitches

Insertion stitches are decorative stitches joining two pieces of material together across a narrow gap. They vary from the very simple to the extremely complicated; three of the more straightforward ones are illustrated here.

The two pieces of fabric to be joined are basted to strips of brown paper or heavy linen, approximately ⅜" (1cm) in from the edges, to hold them in place ready for the embroidery. The strips should be about 2" (5cm) wide and are placed underneath the fabric, allowing the embroidery to be worked on top. For the stitches described below, the size of the gap between the pieces of fabric should be ¼" (5mm) or less, otherwise the embroidery will be loose and unstable. The backing strips are removed once the embroidery is finished.

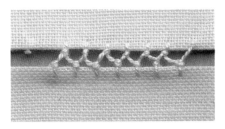

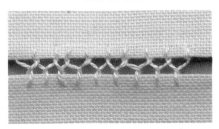

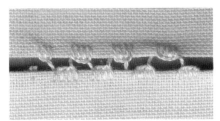

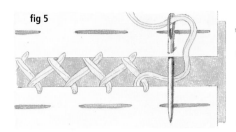

Open Cretan insertion stitch

This is one of the simplest insertion stitches, and the working method is like that of feather stitch (see page 74), the stitches being worked from edge to edge across the gap (fig 5). The distance between the stitches should be as regular as possible.

Knotted insertion stitch

This stitch is worked in the same way as open Cretan insertion stitch, but in addition a chain stitch is made over each loop (fig 6).

Buttonhole insertion stitch

This insertion stitch is made up of groups of buttonhole stitches (usually four), worked alternately on each edge of the fabric (fig 7). The gap between the edges of the fabric should be narrower than for open Cretan insertion stitch and knotted insertion stitch.

When changing from one fabric edge to the other, care must be taken that the cross threads are kept to an even, tight tension, otherwise the groups of buttonhole stitches will lose their shape and become uneven.

fig 5

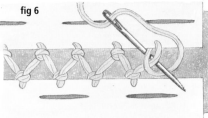

fig 6

fig 7

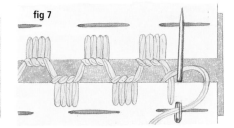

cutwork leaves

Stitches used
running stitch (page 24),
buttonhole stitch (page 36),
buttonhole-stitch bars (page 37),
double buttonhole-stitch bars (page 37).

Cutwork is the name used for embroidery where part of the fabric is cut away after the stitching is finished. Where the pattern is dense, the balance between those areas to be cut and those to be left must be considered. Buttonhole stitch is used for cutwork as it provides a solid edge from which the fabric can be cut away without fear of fraying. Where large areas of fabric are cut, the holes can be reinforced with stitch bars.

This cutwork design uses an informal leaf pattern which can fit virtually any size of panel. The design is illustrated opposite on a delicate tablecloth, but also lends itself to a wide border on a translucent curtain (see page 35). The motifs rather than the background have been cut to accentuate their shapes. Buttonhole-stitch bars and double buttonhole-stitch bars have been incorporated into the design to hold the shapes and prevent them from sagging. It is advisable to use an embroidery hoop when working this piece, as very lightweight fabrics such as organza can easily pucker if hand-held. An alternative cutwork design is given on pages 98–99.

You will need
White organza fabric of the size
   required
Crewel (embroidery) needle size 5
   or 6
Embroidery hoop with stand/clamp
Sharp-pointed embroidery scissors
Coton à broder in DMC 746 or Anchor
   386 (two skeins were used to
   complete the design illustrated)

To prepare the fabric
1 A selection of the leaf shapes used for the cutwork design is given here. The larger leaves have stitch bars.
2 Transfer the leaves to the fabric in a random or repeat pattern, using method 1 or 3 described on pages 16–17. Mark the positions of the stitch bars.

To work the embroidery
1 Mount the fabric in an embroidery hoop. When working the stitching, your right hand should be under the work and your left hand on top (the other way around for left-handed stitchers). If you prefer not to use a frame, take care not to pull the threads tight as this will cause the fabric to pucker.
2 Starting anywhere you wish, work running stitch between the double lines around the leaf shapes, adding bars where indicated. Outline each leaf with buttonhole stitch, making sure that the looped edge of the stitch faces inward.
3 When all the buttonhole stitching and buttonhole-stitch bars are complete, begin cutting out the shapes**.** Using a pair of sharp-pointed embroidery scissors, cut away the fabric from inside the leaves up to the edge of the buttonhole stitching. Take great care not to cut the buttonhole bars by accident as you are doing this.

To finish
Make the finished embroidery into the item of your choice. For a tablecloth, turn under a hem all round, mitering the corners (see page 94). To make a curtain, stitch a channel along the top edge to hold a curtain rod. Hem the lower edge.

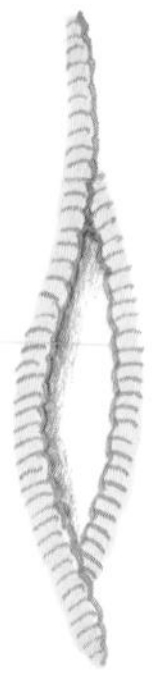

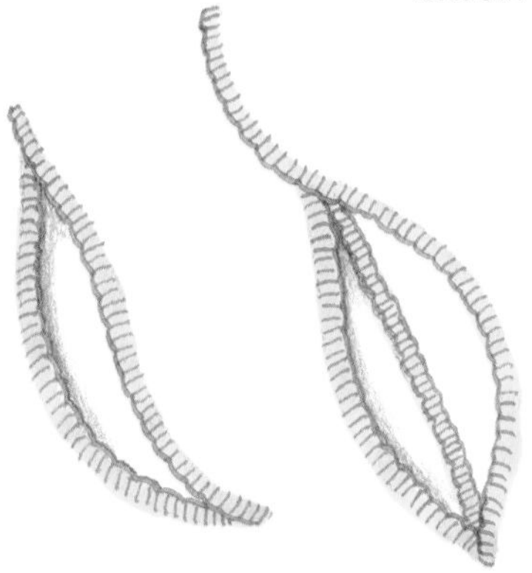

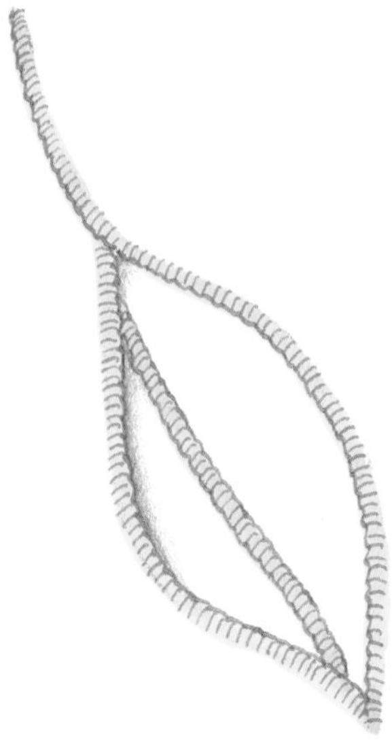

These leaf motifs are shown actual size.
Trace the outlines as double lines and transfer onto the fabric
at random or to form a repeat pattern. Choose either buttonhole-
stitch bars or double buttonhole-stitch bars to bridge the larger leaves.

edged pillowcase

A little openwork embroidery around a pillowcase can transform it from a utilitarian piece of bed linen into a luxury item, and one that can be enjoyed every day. A sheet can be edged in the same way to make a matching set. Adjust the diagram in figure 1 so that the inner rectangle fits your pillow. This type of embroidery is used mainly to decorate bed linen, tablecloths, napkins, hand towels and sheer curtains.

Stitches used
insertion stitch (choose from those on page 39).

fig 1   allow ¹⁄₁₆"/5mm gap for embroidery and 2½"/6cm for folded edging bands

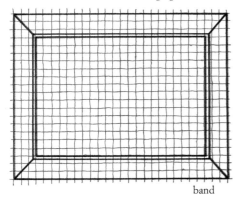

band

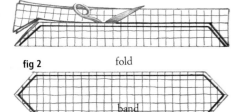

fig 2   fold

band

You will need
For the pillowcase:
Dressmaker's pattern paper
Linen or medium-weight cotton fabric (for quantity, see below)
Matching sewing thread
2 buttons
For the embroidery:
Brown paper, cut into 2" (5cm) strips to length and width of pillowcase
Crewel (embroidery) needle size 4
⅓oz (10g) white pearl cotton no. 8

To make the paper pattern
1 Draw the diagram in fig 1 onto dressmaker's pattern paper. Trace one long and one short band.
2 Fold the pattern paper along the outer edge of the bands, adding ½" (1cm) seam allowance to the ends and inner edge (fig 2). Cut out.
3 Trace the main rectangle, add seam allowances all around, and cut out.

To cut out
1 Cut out two rectangles, making one 1" (3cm) longer than the pattern.
2 Cut a strip of fabric the width of the rectangle and 6" (15cm) wide for a button band.
3 Cut out two short and two long edging bands.

To make the embroidered edging
1 Press each of the edging bands in half lengthwise, right side out. Press the seam allowances on the long sides to the wrong side.

2 Open out the bands and lay the short ones on the long ones, right sides together, matching the ends. Pin and stitch (fig 3). Make the other two mitered corners in the same way. Press all four seams open, then re-fold and press the original folds.
3 Press the seam allowances on the smaller rectangle (pillowcase top) to the wrong side. Pin and baste firmly, right side up, onto the strips of brown paper.
4 Lay the edging band in place around this rectangle, tucking the paper between the two layers of the band. Pin and baste the top layer only of the band to the paper, leaving a ³⁄₁₆" (5mm) gap.
5 Work your chosen insertion stitch all around, filling the gap. Remove the basting threads and paper strips.
6 Pin the underside of the edging band in place on the wrong side, close to the inner edge, and slip stitch in place.

To finish
1 Make a 1½" (3.5cm) hem at one end of the larger rectangle and press the remaining seam allowances to the wrong side. Lay this rectangle on the first one, wrong sides together, pin the unhemmed sides in place, and slip stitch.
2 Press the button band in half lengthwise, right sides out, press the seam allowances all around to the wrong side, and slip stitch these edges together. Make two buttonholes evenly spaced on the button band.
3 Lay the button band on the wrong side of the pillowcase top, at the open end, with the slip stitched long side and ends lying against the edge of the embroidery. Pin and slip stitch.
4 Stitch the buttons to the hem on the other rectangle to match the positions of the buttonholes.

fig 3

43

paisley sampler pillow

The real purpose of a sampler is to allow the embroiderer to practice and experiment with stitches, using the finished work as a reference for future projects. A sampler is therefore more of a "needlework notebook" than a finished, artistic piece, for the mistakes and irregularities are as useful as the perfectly formed stitches. It will show you how a particular effect is achieved, and for this the back of the work is as important as the front for the information it can impart.

This sampler, finished off as a pillow, does not set out to be perfect, but illustrates some of the outline and edging stitches that are discussed in this and the previous chapter, using them both as linear and as filling stitches. Many other stitches can be substituted; use some that you find attractive and would like to experiment with. The color palette is small, which makes it easier to handle. Use all or some of the colors in each shape, selecting them as you go along. This serves to illustrate how colors influence one another and can look quite different when placed close together.

Stitches used
For the paisley outlines:
Buttonhole stitch (page 36).
For the paisley fillings:
running stitch (page 24),
laced running stitch (page 24),
backstitch (page 24),
Pekinese stitch (page 25),
stem stitch (page 25),
chain stitch (page 25),
blanket stitch (page 36).
For the border:
hemstitch, but without
catching a hem (page 38).

You will need
For the pillow:
16" (40cm) square lightweight ticking
fabric for backing
10" (25cm) zipper
Matching sewing thread
12" x 10½" (30 x 27cm) pillow form
For the embroidery:
16" (40cm) square putty-colored
evenweave linen, 20 threads per
1" (2.5cm)
Crewel (embroidery) needles size 6 or 7
for outlining and size 5 for filling
Tapestry needle size 26 for hemstitch
border and laced stitches
Anchor or DMC *coton à broder,* pearl
cotton no. 3 and pearl cotton no. 5
in the colors shown on page 46

To prepare the fabric

Transfer the pattern shown opposite to the fabric using any of the methods described on pages 16–17.

To work the embroidery

1 Outline all the paisley shapes in closely worked buttonhole stitch, using *coton à broder*.

2 Fill the paisley shapes with embroidery, using the stitches shown in the key on the right or a selection of your own. Use pearl cotton no. 5 for this.

3 Draw a rectangle measuring 8¾" x 7½" (22 x 19cm) around the embroidery, extending the lines to the edge of the fabric. Pull out four threads along each of the lines (see page 38). Hemstitch the remaining threads into groups of three threads per stitch, using pearl cotton no. 3.

To finish

1 Using the lightweight ticking fabric, make the basic pillow as described for the Crewelwork Pansies (see page 32) to measure 13" x 12" (33 x 30cm).

2 Iron the pillow cover carefully, right sides out, making sure that the seams create a crisp fold and that the corners are square.

3 Baste the back to the front, about 1" (2cm) from the edge. Machine stitch all around approx ¾" (1.5cm) in from the edge (fig 1), then remove the basting threads. Insert the pillow form.

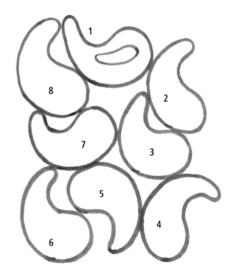

Key to paisley stitches

1 Stem stitch worked in concentric shapes.
2 Blanket stitch worked in linking rows.
3 Backstitch worked in straight lines.
4 Stem stitch and running stitch worked in straight lines.
5 Chain stitch worked in concentric shapes.
6 Pekinese stitch worked in straight lines.
7 Running stitch worked in concentric shapes.
8 Laced running stitch worked in straight lines.

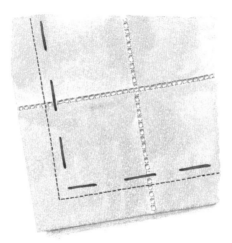

		Anchor	DMC
	Paisley outlines	*Coton à broder*	
■	Slate gray	1035	930
	Paisley fillings	*Pearl cotton no. 5*	
■	Crimson	19	304
■	Magenta	78	601
▥	Soft pink	76	3350
■	Browny pink	1019	315
▨	Terracotta	338	920
	Border	*Pearl cotton no. 3*	
☐	White	2	blanc neige

Quantity

One skein or ball of each color.

fig 1

This pattern is shown actual size. Trace the outlines
of the paisleys only and transfer onto the fabric.
Fill with the stitches shown in the key opposite.

47

Filling with color

Filling stitches are designed to provide coverage, and almost any embroidery stitch can be adapted for use as a filling stitch. Rows of stitching can be closely worked, isolated stitches can be grouped either randomly or in a planned formation, and stitches can be laced with threads to join them together. There is great scope for invention.

The normal use for filling stitches is to "paint in" the shapes in a design. However, just filling in a background while leaving the shapes of a design blank can also be very effective if the shapes are relatively simple. This technique is known as reversing out.

Open filling stitches are those which do not completely cover the fabric and are a useful way of treating large areas for which solid embroidery would look heavy and be laborious to work. Solid filling stitches, on the other hand, provide dense blocks of texture and color, depending on how closely the embroidery is worked, and can be padded underneath to give an extra fullness and richness, a device which is often used to great effect in ecclesiastical embroidery.

filling stitches

The choice of filling stitch in a design depends a lot on the shape of the space or motif to be filled. Large areas, especially backgrounds, are usually worked in relatively open stitches that do not cover the fabric completely. This is not only for speed of execution but also so as not to create an unbalanced design by giving the background undue importance. Denser, and therefore more color-intensive, stitches such as satin stitch or flat stitch are normally best used for smaller shapes such as petals and leaves.

Satin stitch and padded satin stitch

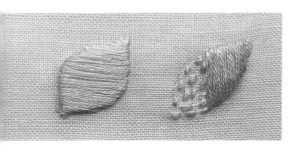

The most commonly used filling stitch is satin stitch, which covers areas with long, smooth stitches placed close together, giving the effect of continuous, solid, smooth color (fig 1). The stitches should be worked from one side to the other, laying them so that no fabric shows through.

If desired, other stitches such as running stitch, or satin stitch worked in a different direction, may be worked first to form a padding underneath, which gives a raised effect for padded satin stitch (figs 2 and 3). Light catching on the curves made by padded satin stitch adds an extra dimension to the density of color that this stitch, above all others, creates.

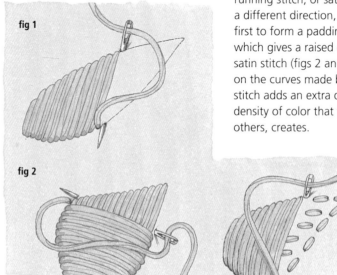

fig 1

fig 2

fig 3

Long and short stitch

This form of satin stitch consists of straight stitches in varying lengths blended into one another. It is often used to fill a shape which is too large or too irregular in outline to be covered by ordinary satin stitch. It can also be used to achieve a shaded effect. In the first row the stitches are alternately long and short and follow the outline of the shape closely (fig 4). The stitches in the following rows are worked to achieve a smooth appearance (fig 5).

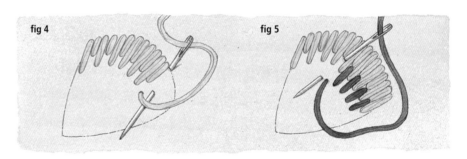

fig 4

fig 5

Flat stitch

Another important filling stitch is flat stitch, which creates a slight crisscross effect down the center of the shape it fills and is good for leaf shapes. Alternatively, it can be divided to go around another stitch (as demonstrated on the Indian Valance on page 64) or it can be stitched in linear form.

1 Start at the top or most pointed end of a shape. If it has a definite point, make a long stitch down from the point first (fig 6). For a linear stitch, bring the thread through on one edge.

2 Work the stitches from side to side, bringing up the thread at the outside edges until the shape is filled. Lines can be drawn inside the shape as a guide to placing the stitches (fig 7).

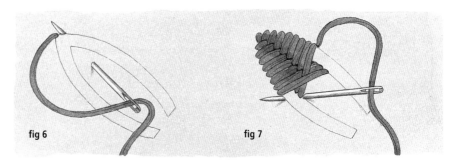

fig 6

fig 7

Cretan stitch

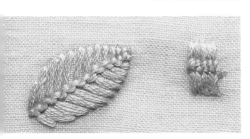

Like flat stitch, Cretan stitch can fill a variety of irregular shapes, or can be worked in linear form. The stitch produces a braided effect down the center of the work.

1 Start at the top or most pointed end of a shape. If it has a definite point, make a long stitch down from the point first. For a linear stitch, bring the thread through as shown in figs 8 and 9.

2 Work the stitches from side to side, taking the thread from the outside edges of the shape to the center. Loop the thread under the needle each time to create the braid.

Fig 10 shows the linear form of the stitch, while figs 11 and 12 show a leaf shape being filled.

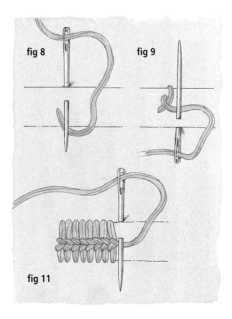

fig 8

fig 9

fig 11

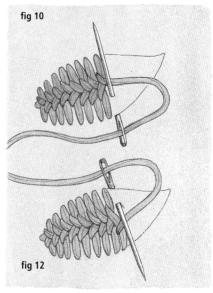

fig 10

fig 12

Cross stitch

Probably the most popular stitch of our time, cross stitch is used for most counted thread work embroidery in which the crosses are all the same size and are joined. However, cross stitch can also be stitched free-form, placed as required and not necessarily joined together.

Cross stitch is frequently used to create pictures, employing the crosses in a "digital" manner – making up pictures through a mass of single stitches of the same size, evenly placed on evenweave fabric. Patterns for cross stitch are often charted on graph paper, and the image is reproduced by counting each stitch as it is worked, following the chart. This is called counted thread work.

When executing cross stitch, it is essential that all the top stitches run in the same direction: if stitched in different directions, they give the work a messy and uneven look. However, reversing the tops of stitches in symmetrical motifs can enhance rather than detract from the piece, but this does need to be planned carefully.

There are two different ways of executing cross stitch. In the first method (figs 1–3), each cross is completed before starting the next one. In the second method (figs 4 and 5), the underneath stitches in each row are all worked first.

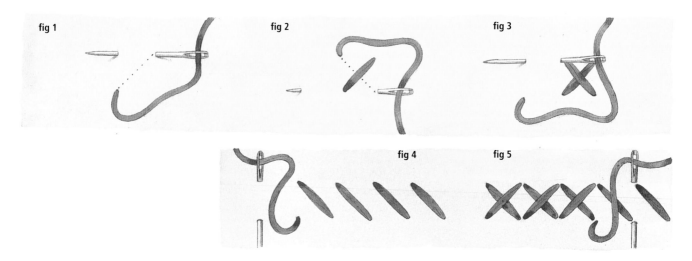

fig 1   fig 2   fig 3

fig 4   fig 5

Double cross stitch

Also known as Leviathan or Smyrna cross stitch, double cross stitch consists of a basic cross stitch as described above, with another cross made over the top in a horizontal and vertical direction. This stitch is more generally used for canvaswork, where all the stitches are necessarily the same length, whereas for embroidery the top cross can be made to whatever size is required – a small top stitch in a contrasting color can be very pretty (figs 6 and 7).

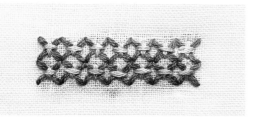

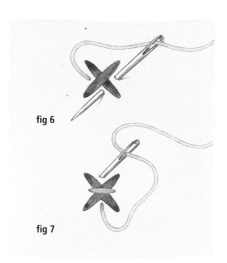

fig 6

fig 7

Couching and Bokhara couching

Couching is the term used for fastening threads in place by securing them with small stitches. Two of the many types of couching are described here.

For the basic couching stitch (fig 8), lay a thread along the line to be embroidered. Using another thread, tie the yarn down with small over-stitches. These can be made in a contrasting color and should be evenly spaced. This stitch can be used both for single lines – stalks, for instance – and for filling open areas. It is often used in goldwork, where the gold threads would not lie flat if stitched through the fabric.

Bokhara couching is different from basic couching in that it uses the same thread both for the under-stitches and the "couching" stitches that hold them down. A long stitch is taken across the shape to be filled, then stitched down with small over-stitches (fig 9).

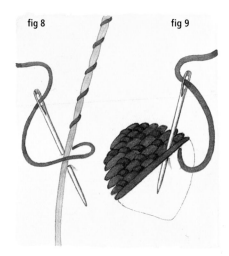

The placement of the couching stitches can be used to form a pattern on the surface. This stitch is useful for filling leaf and petal shapes in the same way as satin stitch does, but it provides more texture and firmness over larger areas.

Cloud stitch

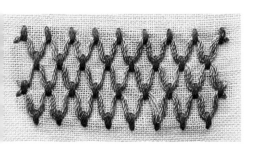

Cloud stitch is an open filling stitch that is quick and pretty. It can be used to fill large areas, and can be effective in geometric designs where only the background is embroidered. In the Crazy Patchwork (page 90), it is used as a linear stitch, with two rows of upright stitches laced together.

1 Make several rows of small, upright, evenly spaced stitches, the spacing alternating with each row.
2 Lace the stitches with a second thread, taking it first under a stitch in the top

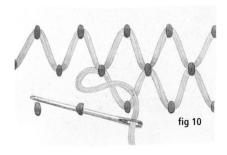

row and then under one in the next row down. Continue working to and fro to fill the space (fig 10).

Seed stitch

Seed stitch – or seeding – is a simple filling stitch composed of small, separated backstitches of equal length (fig 11). Like scattered seeds, they are usually placed at random over an area. Alternatively, they may be stitched in informal patterns, in lines, or following the outlines of a shape. These little stitches are pretty and effective, and give a gentler touch than French knots, which are often used in similar ways to add texture to a design.

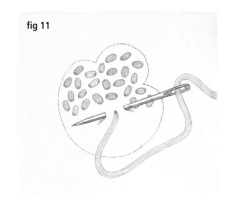

blue-and-white bedspread

The appeal of blue and white is timeless, and this pretty piece has been handed down from generation to generation. It has been used and washed, removing a lot of the original color from the pearl cotton thread but giving it a charming, faded quality that only age and use can provide. Modern threads have better resistance to light, but will still eventually fade somewhat. The embroidery is fairly coarse in texture, which is just as well since a lot of it is now white and would virtually disappear without this added dimension.

The bedspread is made up of a central embroidered panel surrounded by fourteen square pieces, each with the same pattern repeated. These are joined by bands of crochet lace. Each square has been hemmed and the crochet has been stitched on by hand, edge to edge. Strips of ready-made lace may be used instead of the crochet, to equal effect. An alternative design for the bedspread is given on pages 100–101.

Stitches used
satin stitch (page 50),
stem stitch (page 25),
feather stitch (page 74).

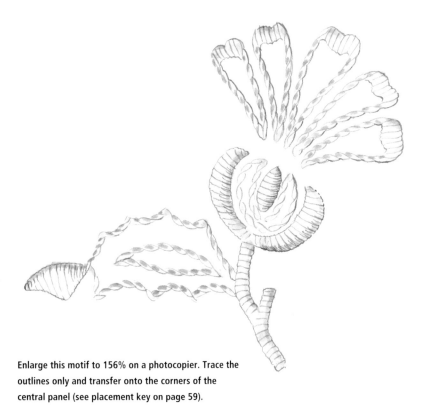

Enlarge this motif to 156% on a photocopier. Trace the outlines only and transfer onto the corners of the central panel (see placement key on page 59).

You will need

For the bedspread:
9yd (8m) lace, 3" (7.5cm) wide, for inserts
5½yd (5m) lace the desired width, for edging
White sewing thread
For the embroidery:
Medium-weight white cotton or linen fabric, 40" (1m) wide x 96" (2.4m) long or 54" (1.4m) wide x 84" (2.1m) long
Crewel (embroidery) needle size 2 or 3
Pearl cotton no. 3, in either the Anchor or DMC colors suggested below

Enlarge these motifs to 156% on a photocopier. Trace the outlines only and transfer onto the central panel. The small motif is placed at each side of the centerpiece. Refer to the placement key on page 59.

		Anchor	DMC
⊔	Pale blue	128 or 144	809 or 3753

Quantity

It is not possible to give exact thread quantities as this project is based on an old piece. Start off with 10 skeins and add more as required.

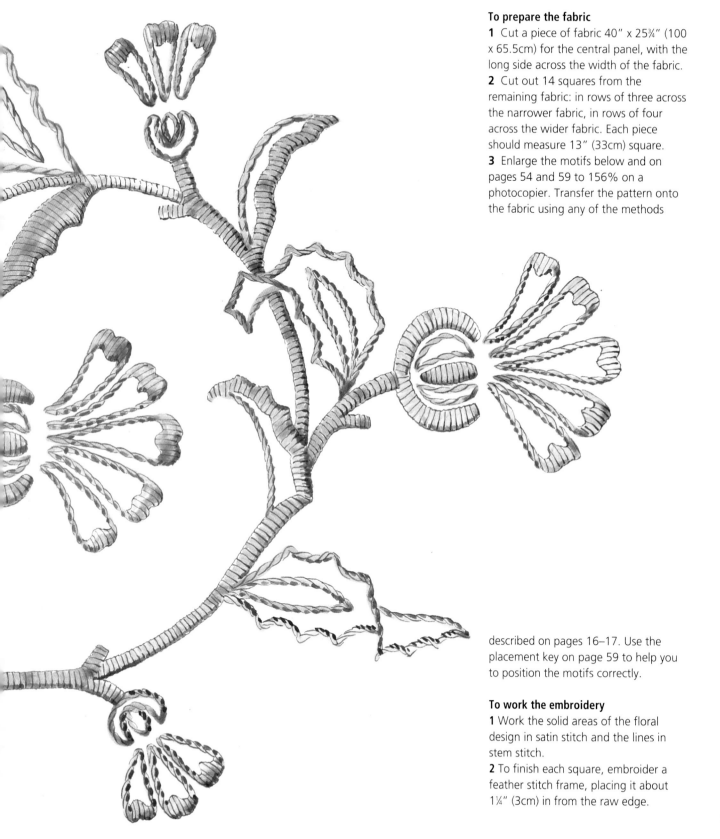

To prepare the fabric

1 Cut a piece of fabric 40" x 25¾" (100 x 65.5cm) for the central panel, with the long side across the width of the fabric.

2 Cut out 14 squares from the remaining fabric: in rows of three across the narrower fabric, in rows of four across the wider fabric. Each piece should measure 13" (33cm) square.

3 Enlarge the motifs below and on pages 54 and 59 to 156% on a photocopier. Transfer the pattern onto the fabric using any of the methods described on pages 16–17. Use the placement key on page 59 to help you to position the motifs correctly.

To work the embroidery

1 Work the solid areas of the floral design in satin stitch and the lines in stem stitch.

2 To finish each square, embroider a feather stitch frame, placing it about 1¼" (3cm) in from the raw edge.

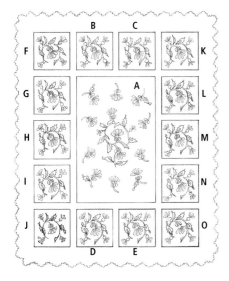

The key above shows the motif positions and the order of sewing up the panels (indicated by letters A–O).

To finish

1 Hem each square so as to create squares with 10½" (27cm) sides. This is best done by hand, but can also be stitched by machine, in which case work the feather stitch embroidery over the top of the machine stitching. Hem the central panel in the same way to measure 37¾" x 24¼" (96 x 61.5cm).

2 To join the pieces together, refer to the placement key on the left. Start with the central panel (A). Cut two strips of lace to fit along the two short sides, allowing for a hem at each end. The hem allowance will depend on the type of lace – heavier lace needs a wider hem than fine lace. Hem the ends and machine stitch to the panel.

3 Take two of the squares (B and C) and join with a lace panel in between, as above. Repeat with squares D and E.

4 Sew these two pieces to the top and bottom of the central panel (A).

5 Sew a strip of lace to each of the long sides of the central panel and squares to create the central section of the bedspread.

6 Take five more squares (F to J) and join with lace panels in between, as above. Repeat for the remaining five squares (K to O).

7 Sew these pieces to each side of the central section created in step 5.

8 Sew the remaining lace around the outer edge to complete the bedspread, gathering it at the corners.

Enlarge this motif to 156% on a photocopier. Trace the outlines only and transfer onto the 14 fabric squares which surround the central panel (see placement key above).

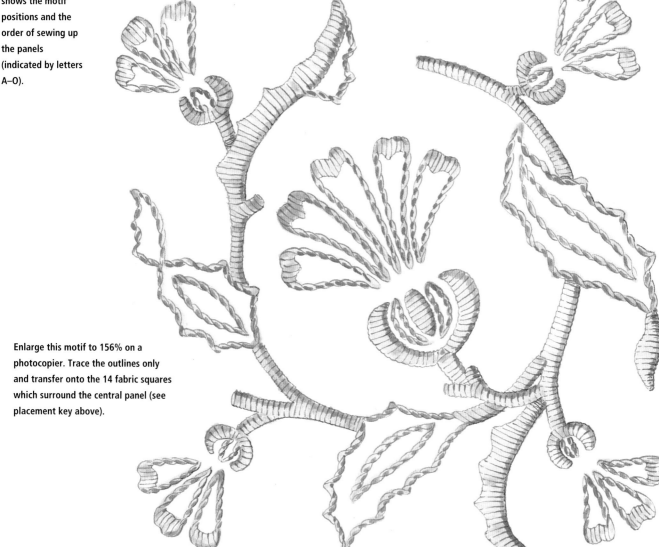

floral tea cozy and tablecloth

Stitches used
padded satin stitch (page 50),
long and short stitch (page 50),
stem stitch (page 25),
lazy daisy stitch (page 75),
seed stitch (page 53),
French knots (page 76),
drawn thread work (page 38).

Tea cozies may be reminders of the past – a relic of times when houses were unheated and maids did the laundry – but they are still appealing as decorative accessories for special occasions. For embroiderers, they offer a small and achievable project that is not difficult to sew together once the embroidery has been completed. Here, the embroidered tea cozy is treated as a detachable cover for a padded cozy for ease of washing.

This design uses mainly padded satin stitch, along with some seed stitch and lazy daisy stitches, among others. The choice of such deep shades of yellow, rust, pink, and green, and an unexpected blue, makes a particularly strong color statement which is the first thing you notice about the design. Note the carefully planned direction in which the stitches are laid, creating important color variation through the way in which light falls on the thread.

The same floral pattern has been used to make a matching tablecloth (shown opposite, and also on page 21 where it has been made up into a bolster cover), but it can be adapted for a wide variety of other projects too.

Tea cozy

You will need

For the tea cozy:
Tissue paper, for template
1yd (1m) square piece cotton or linen
Sewing thread
2 pieces heavyweight wadding, each
16½" x 11" (42 x 29cm)
For the embroidery:
2 pieces fine evenweave linen, each
17¾" x 12½" (45 x 32cm)
Crewel (embroidery) needle size 7
Anchor or DMC cotton floss in the
colors shown on page 63

To work the embroidery

1 The two motifs provided below and on page 63 are for the back and front of the cozy. Enlarge them to 116% on a photocopier. Trace and transfer the patterns onto the fabric using any of the methods described on pages 16–17. The colors of cotton floss to use for each part of the embroidery are shown in the key given on page 63.

2 Start stitching in the middle, working the large flowers first and moving outward. From the photograph, note carefully the directions in which the

Use this motif on the back of the tea cozy.
Enlarge to 116% on a photocopier, then trace the
outlines only and transfer onto the fabric.

padded satin stitch and long and short stitch should run on each part of the embroidery, as these are important in achieving the full color impact. Work the stems, leaf veins, and stamens in stem stitch. Add some of the flower centers in French knots and use seed stitch for the center of the large blue-and-white flower.

To finish the cozy

1 Make a tissue paper template of the shape of the finished cozy: for the cozy illustrated, this will be 16½" (42cm) wide by 11" (29cm) high. Mark these two measurements on the tissue paper and draw the curve freehand, starting at the center top (fig 1). When you have drawn one half to your satisfaction, cut it out and fold it over to draw around for the other half.

2 Pin the template to the embroidered linen pieces, making sure that the embroidery is placed correctly, and cut out. Using the same template, cut four lining pieces, and then two pieces of wadding to match.

3 With right sides of the embroidered pieces together, machine stitch a ⅝" (1.5cm) seam along the curve. Do the same for both pairs of lining pieces, but this time increase the seam allowance to ¾" (2cm). Press.

4 Turn one of the linings right side out and put the second one inside. Push the two pieces of wadding in between the layers. Turn under the bottom edges of both linings and hand sew together. Make a few random quilting stitches right through the lining and wadding to hold the wadding in place. Simply work a few stitches in each place and secure – do not run the threads from one place to the next.

5 Finish the edge of the embroidered cozy with drawn thread work (see page 38) or a plain hem. Place over the padded under-cozy.

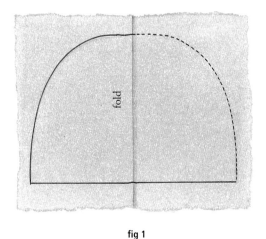

fig 1

Tablecloth

1 To use the design for a tablecloth, plan the placement of the motifs on the tablecloth (which could be a ready-made one) before you start (see page 16 for guidance). The extra motif, stitched in gold at the corners of the tablecloth, is supplied below.

2 Work the embroidery as for the tea cozy. The extra gold motif is worked in satin stitch and stem stitch.

This motif for the corners of the tablecloth is shown actual size. Trace the outlines only and transfer onto the fabric.

Quantity

For the tea cozy, one skein of each color should be sufficient. You may need more skeins of thread for the tablecloth, depending on how many motifs you choose to repeat.

NB Use three strands of Anchor or DMC cotton floss throughout, except for the stems and leaf outlines, for which only two strands are used.

		Anchor	DMC			Anchor	DMC
	Pale blue	130	809		Rust	1049	921
	Mid blue	145	799		Dark rust	339	919
	Aquamarine	185	747		Mushroom	832	841
	Pale mauve	85	3609		Mid green	240	470
	Mauve	86	3608		Leaf green	225	989
	Pale pink	74	3689		Dark olive green	281	581
	Mid pink	25	604		Yellow	288	445
	Dark pink	76	962		Gold	306	743
	Magenta	88	3607		White	2	blanc neige

Use this motif on the front of the tea cozy. Enlarge to 116% on a photocopier, then trace the outlines only and transfer onto the fabric.

indian valance

The pattern for this valance is taken straight from the border of an Indian bedspread, probably stitched by a bride to impress her husband with her abilities. In this instance, the whole bedspread is embroidered using flat stitch only, suggesting that perhaps her talents were limited after all. However, the use of color is exciting, and the design – possibly not the bride's own – is lively and beautiful.

Traditionally in the West, neutral backgrounds for embroidery have been favored to the extent that other options are rarely considered. Here, however, ticking has been used as the base fabric for the valance, illustrating how bold embroidery can sit very happily on a patterned background. When buying the ticking, add 20 per cent to the width you require – this will give a gentle gather. The depth should be at least 10" (25cm).

Stitches used
flat stitch (page 51),
stem stitch (page 25),
backstitch (page 24),
straight stitch (page 75).

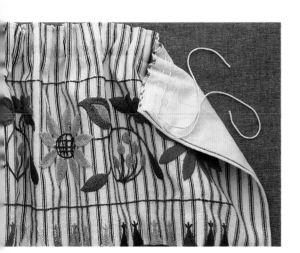

You will need
For the valance:
Curtain gathering tape, same length as
  finished embroidery
White sewing thread
Stapler or touch-and-close fastening
For the embroidery:
Good-quality lightweight ticking to
  required size (see above)
Crewel (embroidery) needle size 5
Embroidery hoop frame
Anchor or DMC cotton floss in the
  colors shown on page 67

To work the embroidery
1 Enlarge the pattern on pages 66–67 to 112% on a photocopier. Trace and transfer onto the fabric using method 2 or method 3 described on pages 16–17.
2 Start stitching at one end and work the embroidery across the fabric, motif by motif. Stitch the flowers, stems, and jade leaves first, then fill in the other motifs. Use flat stitch for the solid areas, stem stitch for the stems, and backstitch for the narrow border lines. Top each triangle along the lower edge with three

straight stitches. It is advisable to use an embroidery hoop when working flat stitch, especially for the larger motifs, as otherwise the fabric can easily be pulled out of shape.

To finish

1 Turn over and press the fabric 2¼" (5.5cm) above the top backstitch line of the embroidery. Pin and baste the gathering tape to the back of the

embroidery along the fold. Machine stitch along the top and bottom of the tape.

2 Hem the bottom edge of the valance by hand or machine, 2¼" (5.5cm) from the bottom backstitch line of the embroidery.

3 Pull the gathering thread until the embroidery is the length required.

4 Fix the valance in place using staples, or touch-and-close fastening.

Two different colorways for the valance motif are shown below. Enlarge the repeat pattern to 112% on a photocopier and join where indicated. Trace the outlines only and transfer onto the fabric, repeating as many times as required.

Quantity

It is difficult to be precise about thread quantities, as this depends on how closely you work the stitches and on your choice of colors as you work along. However, as a rough guide, each large flower uses approximately 6½yd (6m) of thread, the curling stem uses 1¾yd (1.5m) per repeat, and the jade green leaves require 4¼yd (4m) per repeat. The best way to manage the quantities is to stitch the flowers, stems, and jade leaves first. Use what remains of the colors to fill in.

NB Use all six strands of floss throughout, except for the stem stitch curling stem, and the small, bright green leaves: only three strands are used here.

		Anchor	DMC
■	Deep purple	119	333
■	Wine red	70	3685
■	Bright red	47	321
▨	Pink	75	962
▨	Light blue	144	800
■	Royal blue	143	797
■	Bright green	238	702
■	Jade green	18	943
▨	Yellow	293	727

cross stitch curtain

Stitches used
cross stitch, worked over three fabric
threads (page 52),
drawn thread and pulled thread work
(pages 38 and 39).

This charming piece was found in an antique market in Massachusetts, and its origins are unknown. Although originally worked on a tablecloth, the interest is confined to the edges, so using the design for a curtain shows off the cross-stitch embroidery to better advantage.

The design uses a simple palette of colors in a repeating pattern. These colors are unsophisticated, as is the stitch configuration, but the effect they produce is fresh and appealing. It could be stitched from the leftover odds and ends that embroiderers always have in their workbaskets, or formally planned to fit into a particular color scheme. The important thing is to use just one color for the leaves to hold the design together, and to choose two heavily contrasting colors for each flower. These flowers have obviously been stitched from the same counted cross stitch pattern, but "mistakes" have been made so that some flowers are slightly different, adding interest to the piece – relentless repeats can be tiring on the eye.

		Anchor	DMC
	Green	238	702
	Purple	92	553
	Orange	316	741
	Yellow	306	743
	Duck egg blue	1039	519
	Prussian blue	169	806
	Dark blue	139	797
	Bright pink	52	962
	Crimson	799	304

Quantity

One skein of each color should stitch approximately four complete flowers and 15 green leaf repeats.

NB Use three strands of thread throughout.

You will need

Evenweave linen, 36 threads per 1" (2.5cm), 6" (15cm) larger than finished curtain all around
Matching sewing thread
Crewel (embroidery) needle size 8
Anchor or DMC cotton floss in the colors shown on the left

To work the embroidery

1 This design is worked from the chart below. Unlike most counted work, where the pattern must be measured meticulously to fit the fabric, the repeat is small enough and the design sufficiently informal to make this unnecessary.

2 Place the cross stitch border about 3½" (9cm) away from the raw edges of the evenweave linen. Start stitching at a corner and work in a continuous line until the next corner is reached, then turn in the best way you can – identical turns are not important to this design. Two possible corner turns are shown on the chart below.

To finish

1 The curtain has been finished with a combination of drawn thread work (center line) with a line of pulled thread work (pin stitch) on each side, stitched with sewing thread. First turn under a 1⅜" (3.5cm) hem and secure with a line of pin stitch. Then work the line of drawn thread work above it and finish off with another line of pin stitch.

2 Hang the curtain from two hooks positioned on either side of the window frame. Catch up the center of the lower edge and sew to the middle of the curtain, hiding the join with a button.

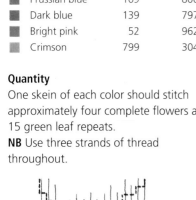

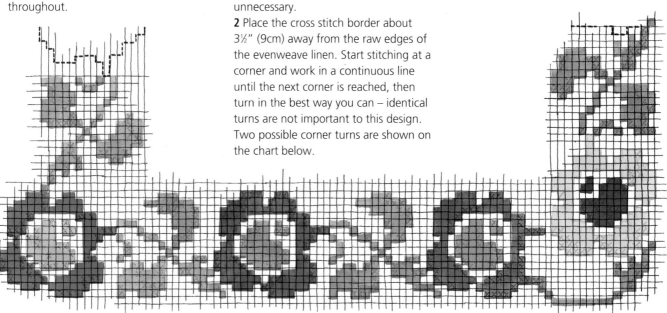

handkerchief sachet

Stitches used
buttonhole stitch (page 36),
satin stitch (page 50),
stem stitch (page 25).

Handkerchief sachets are hardly high on the list of necessities nowadays, but the old-fashioned prettiness of this design – its delicacy of form and surprising strength of color – appeals to most embroiderers. Its simplicity is deceptive, for the construction of the design is clever and takes into account the transparency of the fabric.

The flower stitches have been chosen to ensure that threads need not be carried across the back at any stage, as they would show through. Tightly worked buttonhole stitch is used both for the seam and for edging, eliminating any need for turning under the fabric, which would spoil the light effect. Finally, the front edges are scalloped in a symmetrical wave pattern, which has been designed to accommodate the corners more gracefully than the more usual, even curves of a scalloped cutwork edge.

		Anchor	DMC
☐	Yellow	300	745
■	Orange	303	742
■	Dark coral	9	352
■	Mauve	95	554
■	Blue	136	799
■	Pale blue	975	828
■	Green	205	912
■	Pale green	219	564
Buttonhole stitch edging			
■	Peacock blue	1039	807

Quantity
One skein of each color.
NB Use two strands of thread throughout, except for the stem stitch lines, for which four strands are used.

You will need
12" x 24" (30 x 60cm) approx pale
    green organdy
Spray starch
Sheet of cardboard
Embroidery hoop frame
Crewel (embroidery) needle size 7
Anchor or DMC cotton floss in the
    colors shown on the left

To prepare the fabric
1 Press the fabric, using plenty of spray starch to keep it firm.
2 Pin the fabric out onto a piece of cardboard, so that it does not move while you are transferring the design.
3 Enlarge the design below to 178% on a photocopier. Transfer using method 3 described on pages 16–17, ignoring the markings A. Take care to place the design on the fabric at one end, leaving enough fabric to make the pocket part of the sachet once the embroidery on the front is complete (see To make up, step 1).

To work the embroidery
An embroidery hoop is recommended for working this embroidery, as the fabric is so flimsy that it will pucker easily if held in the hand. It is important always to start and finish threads neatly, as any loose ends will show through.
1 Embroider the flowers first in buttonhole stitch and satin stitch, using the photograph opposite as a guide.
2 Work the rest of the design, including the leaves, in satin stitch.
3 Work the stem stitch line to cover any uneven ends to the leaves.
4 Work the buttonhole scalloped edge for the front flap, but do not trim off the fabric yet.

To finish
1 From the points marked A on the pattern, draw a rectangle 15" (38cm) by 7½" (19cm) wide approximately – the width will be dictated by the placing of the scallop embroidery. Fold this up by 6¼" (16cm) to make the pocket.
2 Buttonhole stitch along the pocket top.
3 Baste the edges of the pocket and buttonhole stitch them together.
4 Trim away the fabric from all the buttonhole stitched edges.

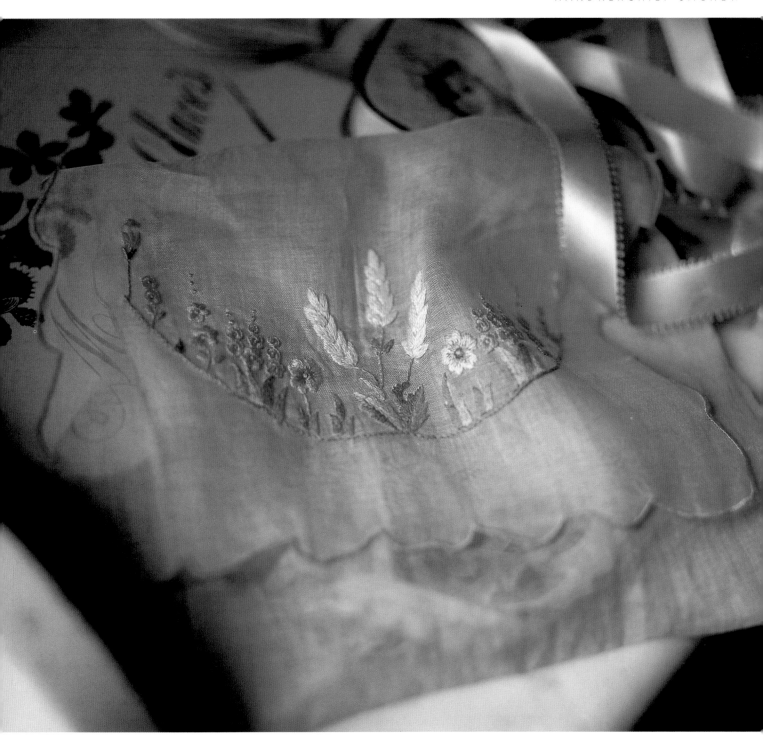

Embroidered embellishments

Embellishment stitches are there for the purpose of simple or elaborate adornment and decoration of fabric. This chapter explores both a single stitch, single color, restrained form of embellishment in the Shell Pillows project on page 78, and at the other extreme the exuberance of the Crazy Patchwork on page 90, where large numbers of both stitches and colors are combined to adorn an already richly decorative piece. In crazy patchwork, every opportunity can be used to show off embroidery techniques, including mementos, dates, and names, by filling in the irregular shapes of the patches with ever more inventive stitches.

Somewhere in between lies the highly creative Beetle Pillow design on page 82, where stitches are used both to delineate and to decorate the

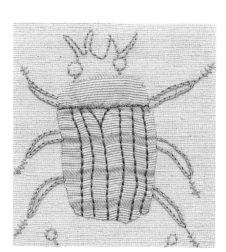

beetles. The clever use of embroidery over the already patterned fabrics of their bodies is a wonderfully free style of expression in stitching.

embellishment stitches

Having learned the basic techniques, the embroiderer may now run free and create endless combinations – straight stitches with French knots, laced and graduated stitches, stitches that interweave – to make an embroidery a truly personal expression of his or her creativity. Linear stitches, such as feather, Cretan, and running stitches, can be decorated with isolated stitches such as French knots, lazy daisy, and straight stitch.

The term "embellishment stitches" can be used to describe almost all embroidery stitches, for they are usually there for the purpose of decoration. Some of the stitches included in this chapter are versions of those that have been described earlier in the book, such as buttonhole and Cretan stitches. They have been chosen to illustrate how, with different treatments, they can become more decorative. Embellishment stitches are where the fun really begins for an adventurous embroiderer.

Feather stitch and double feather stitch

Feather stitch is quick to do and has many variations. Just two are shown here. The stitch is linear in form and is used for many purposes including the embellishment of hems and borders, to imitate sprays of feathery foliage, and to cover seams on crazy patchwork pieces.

1 Bring the needle up through the fabric at (a). Holding the thread down with the left thumb, insert the needle at (b) and take a small stitch down to the center (c), keeping the thread under the needle (fig 1).

2 Insert the needle again at (d) and take a small stitch down to the center, as in step 1. Continue making stitches alternately to right and left of the line.

For double feather stitch (fig 2), two stitches are made alternately to the right and to the left of the line.

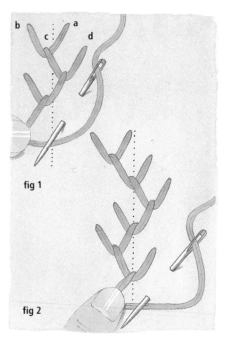

fig 1

fig 2

Open Cretan stitch

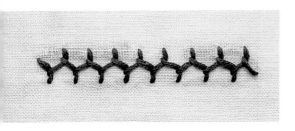

This is a linear stitch and is worked from side to side. The stitches should be evenly spaced to look neat. Akin to feather stitch, it makes good borders and frames. Worked closely, it is an effective filling stitch that gives a slightly braided look (see Cretan stitch, page 51).

1 Bring the needle up through the fabric at (a) and down at (b).

2 Bring the needle up at (c), passing it over the first long stitch. Take the needle down again at (d) and out at (e) (fig 3). Repeat along the design line to form a zigzag band (fig 4).

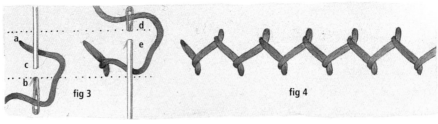

fig 3

fig 4

Straight stitch

Sometimes known as single satin stitch, this is simply a straight stitch. It can be used to create stars (fig 5), fans (fig 6), squares (fig 7), or straight lines, or to add small details such as antennae and feet on the Beetle Pillow (see page 82).

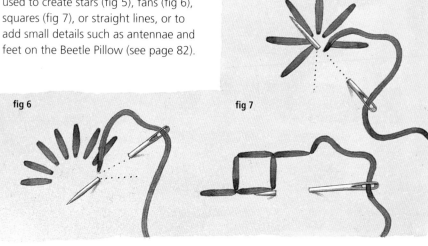

Lazy daisy stitch

Also known as detached chain stitch, this is often one of the first stitches that children learn. It is derived from chain stitch (see page 25), but here each stitch stands alone and is secured by a small stitch at the top of the loop (figs 8 and 9). This stitch can be worked singly, or in groups to form daisy-like petals.

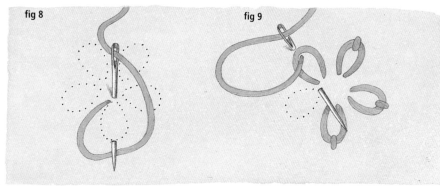

Fly stitch

This versatile stitch is worked in a similar way to lazy daisy stitch (above), but the loops are left open. Fly stitches can be used singly, in rows (fig 10) or in vertical bands (fig 11), and can be placed close together or spaced apart.

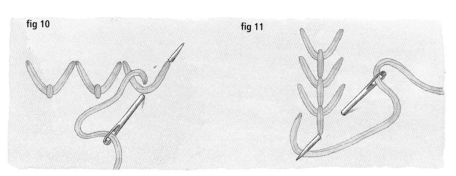

Herringbone stitch

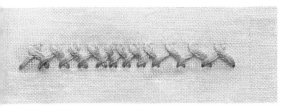

This aptly named stitch is worked in lines and is particularly useful for creating embroidered borders and for covering seams where pieces of fabric have been joined together. It can be closely worked to provide coverage or it can be more widely spaced, and it is very quick to do. It is made up of slanting stitches which cross alternately at the top and bottom of the line of stitching. The best effect is achieved when the angles of the stitches and the spacing are uniform.

1 Starting at the bottom of the line, bring the needle up through the fabric. Insert the needle at the top of the stitch, a little to the right, taking a small stitch to the left (fig 1).

2 Insert the needle at the bottom of the line, a little to the right, taking a small stitch to the left (fig 2).

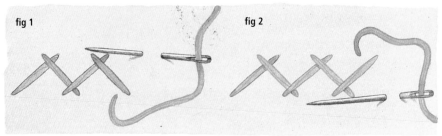

fig 1

fig 2

French knots

These small knots are delightful and lend themselves to a variety of uses. They can provide focus to the centers of flowers, especially when used as an accent color. They make little dots which accentuate shapes, and when scattered over the top of stitches can soften a hard edge or an uncompromising line. French knots can be stitched in clumps, touching one another to give a solid surface, or spaced out, creating a spotty effect.

1 Bring the needle up through the fabric where you want the knot to be.

2 With the needle pointing away from you but keeping it close to the fabric, encircle the thread around it once or twice depending on how large you want the knot to be.

3 Twist the needle around (see arrow in fig 3) and push back through the fabric where the thread originally emerged, keeping the thread tight with the left thumb (fig 4).

4 Pull the thread through sharply. The knot will be left on the top.

If the thread disappears without a knot being achieved, you have encircled the thread the wrong way around the needle in step 2.

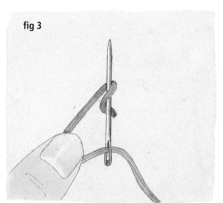

fig 3

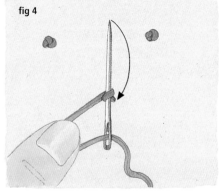

fig 4

Chevron stitch and double chevron stitch

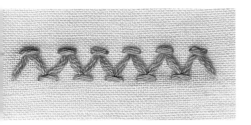

Chevron stitch is a linear stitch and, like herringbone stitch, is worked between a top and bottom line, usually from left to right. It can also be worked "double" – a second row being stitched over the top in a different color, filling the spaces in between the stitches of the first row (see Crazy Patchwork, pages 90–93).

1 Starting on the lower line, bring the thread up and make a stitch along the line with the needle emerging again halfway along the stitch.

2 Slightly to the right, insert the needle into the top line and make a small stitch to the left (fig 5). Make a horizontal stitch to the right, emerging again halfway back along the stitch (fig 6). Repeat, alternating the horizontal stitches between the top and bottom lines to create a zigzag effect.

For double chevron stitch, use exactly the same method to fill in the gaps, keeping the stitches placed centrally over the previous row (fig 7).

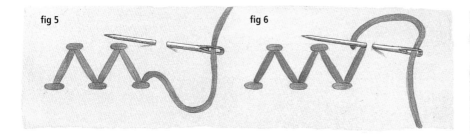

fig 5   fig 6   fig 7

Closed buttonhole stitch

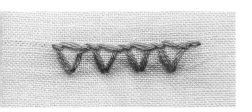

Closed buttonhole stitch (which would be better described as closed blanket stitch) is a simple variation of blanket stitch where the stitches are angled so that each pair creates a small triangle, making it more decorative than plain blanket stitch.

1 Start in the same way as for blanket stitch (see page 36) by bringing the thread up just above the edge of the fabric to anchor it firmly. Work the stitch from left to right.

fig 8

2 Continue as for blanket stitch, slanting the first stitch to the right. Slant the next stitch in the opposite direction (fig 8).

Graduated buttonhole stitch

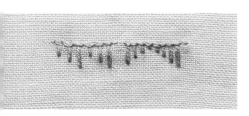

Another way to enhance blanket or buttonhole stitches is to grade the length of the stitches to create different decorative effects such as waves, triangles (fig 9), scallops (fig 10), or steps along the line of stitching.

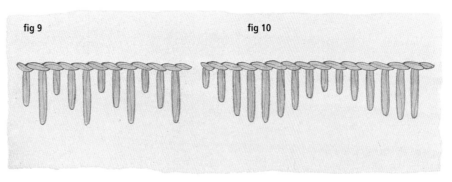

fig 9   fig 10

shell pillows

Stitches used:
French knots (page 76),
backstitch (page 24).

White thread used on white fabric is commonly known as whitework, regardless of the embroidery technique employed. In the absence of color, texture takes on a new importance, whether in the thread, the stitches, or a combination of the two, for it is the shadows that the stitches cast which enable the eye to see the pattern. For this reason, white embroidery often employs cutwork and pulled and drawn thread patterning.

The two stitches chosen for these pillows are French knots, which give plenty of texture, and backstitch, which looks bumpy when stitched with thick, soft cotton thread. One of the pillows is stitched on a blue background to set the embroidery off to more dramatic effect. The background is filled with knots, the shell pattern being created by the spaces left in between. The most important thing to check when choosing a fabric for French knots is that it is woven tightly enough in relation to the yarn used to ensure that the knots do not pull through to the back of the fabric. More shell motifs, which can be arranged in repeating patterns, are given on page 102.

To form the shell design on the blue pillow, repeat the pattern given on page 103 as shown here.

You will need

For each pillow:
18" (45cm) square backing fabric
14" (35cm) zipper
18" (45cm) square pillow form
Fringe trimming (optional)
For the embroidery:
18" (45cm) square white or blue cotton fabric
Chenille needle size 22
Five 11yd (10m) skeins white soft embroidery cotton for the white pillow and eight 11yd (10m) skeins for the blue pillow

To prepare the fabric (blue pillow)

1 The pattern for the shell design on the blue cushion is given on page 103. It is a repeating pattern of lines of identical shells, drawn back to back, so it can be adjusted to fit the required pillow size.

2 Trace the pattern in the center of a piece of tracing paper about 20" (50cm) square. Move the pattern around until you have four vertical lines of shells measuring about 15½" (39cm) square.
3 Transfer the pattern onto the fabric using method 3 described on pages 16–17.

To prepare the fabric (white pillow)

1 The pattern shown on page 81 is a quarter of the complete circle. Enlarge to 133% on a photocopier. Draw 14" (35cm) horizontal and vertical lines intersecting on a piece of tracing paper no smaller than 20" (50cm) square.
2 Trace the pattern four times, once into each of the four sections, making sure that the central point of the pattern and of the tracing paper are aligned each time. This will create the full circle.
3 Transfer the tracing onto the white cotton fabric using method 1 described on page 16.

To work the embroidery

1 Work the French knots before starting the backstitch patterning. As French knots are so exposed, threads must always be started and finished by weaving the thread into a few stitches at the back of the work (see page 18). To start the first stitch of the embroidery, leave a long thread at the back and weave it in when several stitches have been completed.

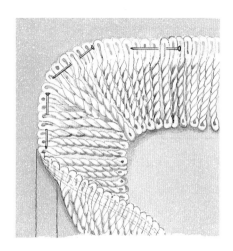

To finish the pillows

1 Insert the zipper into the backing fabric as described for the Crewelwork Pansies on page 32.

2 Place the embroidery face down on a clean, flat surface. Draw a 16" (41cm) square around the worked embroidery: this is the stitching line. Draw curves on the corners – an upturned teacup makes a good template for the corners on the white pillow. The blue pillow has bigger curves, drawn around a saucer.

3 If trimming the pillow with fringing, draw another pencil line ⅜" (1cm) outside the existing line and pin the trimming along it. Ease it around the curves to give plenty of fullness (fig 1).

4 With right sides together, machine stitch the front to the back, with the fringe in between, ⅜" (1cm) from the edge of the fringe. If you are not using fringe, machine stitch the front to the back along the original pencil line.

5 Trim the seam allowance to ¾" (2cm). Snip closer across the corners, taking care not to snip the fringe, if used.

6 Turn the pillow cover right side out and insert the pillow form.

fig 1

A quarter of the shell design for the white pillow is shown here. Enlarge it to 133% on a photocopier, then trace and transfer onto the fabric as described on page 78.

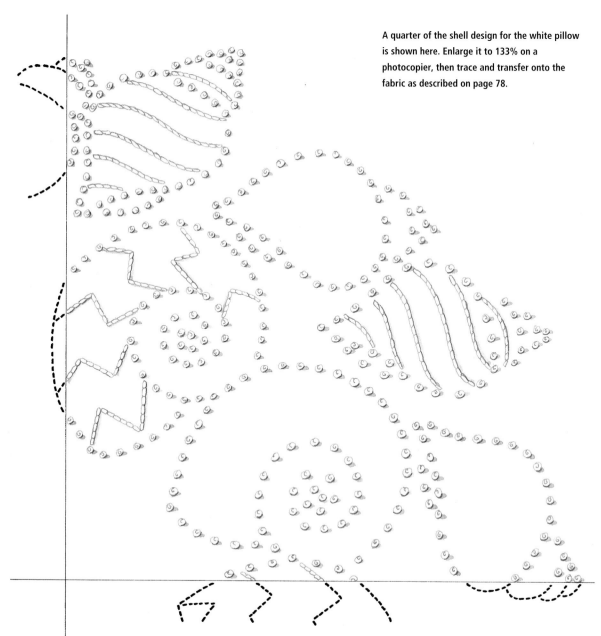

beetle pillow

This modern design is worked in appliqué and embroidery using a variety of stitches. Accuracy is unimportant – it is the free use of the stitcher's imagination and the sheer fun of the subject that give the pillow such vitality. The informality of the design of the individual beetles, combined with the formality of the straight lines in which they are arranged, is a clever juxtaposition of ideas. The appliqué pieces are made from cotton fabrics – each one with an individual stripe – laid at different angles to suggest patterning on the beetles' backs. Some other appliqué motifs are given on page 104.

Stitches used
backstitch (page 24),
chain stitch (page 25),
straight stitch (page 75),
French knots (page 76),
double cross stitch (page 52).

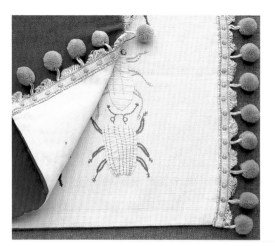

You will need

For the pillow:
20" x 28" (50 x 70cm) royal blue cotton furnishing fabric, for backing
16" (40cm) zipper
1¼yd (1m) bobble trimming
18" x 25" (45 x 65cm) rectangular pillow form

For the embroidery and appliqué:
20" x 28" (50 x 70cm) oatmeal cotton furnishing fabric
12 pieces thin patterned cotton of your choice, each one a minimum of 4" (10cm) square
Stiff tracing paper for templates
Sewing thread to match appliqués
Crewel (embroidery) needle size 5, for embroidery
Sharps needle size 8, for appliqué
Anchor or DMC cotton floss in the colors shown on pages 84 and 86

To prepare the appliqué

1 Trace the shape of each of the 12 beetle bodies on pages 84–87 onto stiff tracing paper and cut them out.
2 Pin each beetle shape onto a cotton square. Cut out around the shapes, leaving a margin of ⅜" (1cm).
3 Turn under the margins and baste in place, sewing through the tracing paper (fig 1). Press well, using a steam iron.
4 Arrange all 12 beetles as desired on the oatmeal fabric. Pin each one on roughly.
5 One by one, remove the basting and tracing paper template and hand sew each beetle in position.

To work the embroidery

1 Transfer the legs and antennae using method 3 described on pages 16–17.
2 Work the embroidery on each beetle following the stitch and color guides on pages 84 and 86. The number of strands used is a matter of personal preference. The French knots and body markings are mostly worked with two or three strands, the legs often with more. Experiment and see what you like.

To finish

1 Make up the pillow, inserting the zipper as given for the Crewelwork Pansies on page 32.
2 Hand sew the bobble trim to both ends of the pillow.

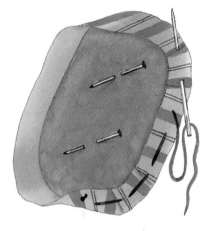

fig 1

		Anchor	DMC
■	Charcoal	400	413
■	Very dark green	862	934
▨	Bronze	906	829
▨	Pale olive	842	3013
▨	Pale aquamarine	875	503
▨	Airforce blue	850	926
□	Pale yellow	300	677

Quantity

One skein of each color

	Stitch	Color
Beetle 1		
Dots on back	French knots	Pale olive
Head and back line	Backstitch	Very dark green
Legs	Chain stitch	Bronze
Eyes and antennae	Backstitch	Pale aqua
Beetle 2		
Back lines	Backstitch	Pale aqua
Legs	Chain stitch	Pale olive
Feet	Small straight stitches over backstitch	Pale olive
Head	Backstitch	Pale olive
Beetle 3		
Back lines and eyes	Backstitch	Pale olive
Dots on back	French knots	Pale yellow
Legs	Chain stitch	Very dark green
Feet and antennae	Small straight stitches over backstitch	Very dark green
Beetle 4		
Back lines and antennae	Backstitch	Pale aqua
Back pattern	Backstitch	Charcoal
Legs	Chain stitch	Bronze
Feet	Small straight stitches over chain stitch	Bronze
Beetle 5		
Back lines	Backstitch	Very dark green
Legs	Chain stitch	Airforce blue
Eyes	Backstitch	Charcoal
Head	Backstitch	Airforce blue
Feet	Backstitch	Airforce blue
Beetle 6		
Back pattern	Backstitch and French knots	Pale yellow
Back circles and antennae	Backstitch	Pale olive
Legs	Chain stitch	Charcoal
Feet	Straight stitches over backstitch	Charcoal

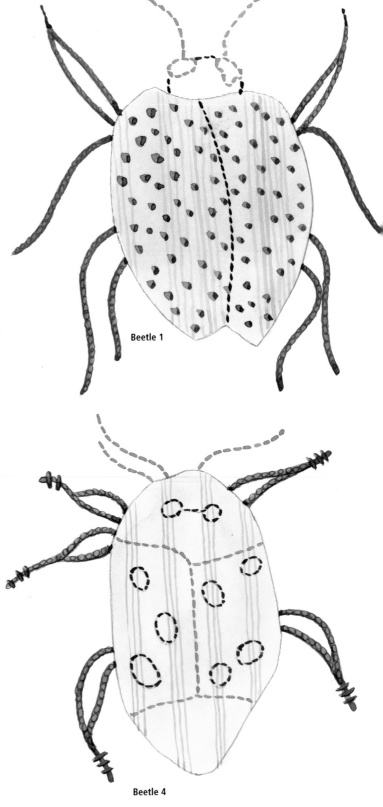

Beetle 1

Beetle 4

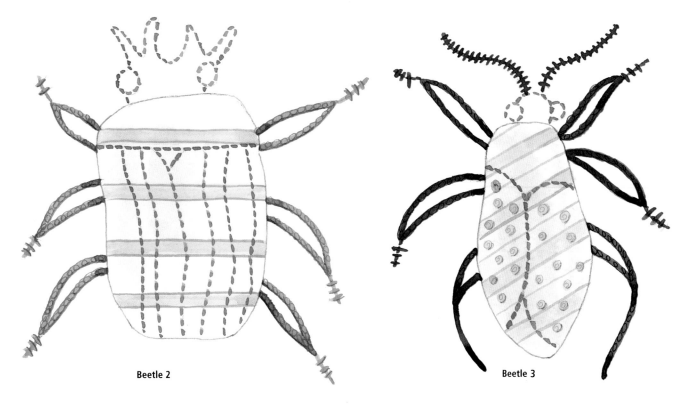

Beetle 2

Beetle 3

These beetle shapes are shown actual size. Trace the bodies onto stiff tracing paper and cut out to use as templates.

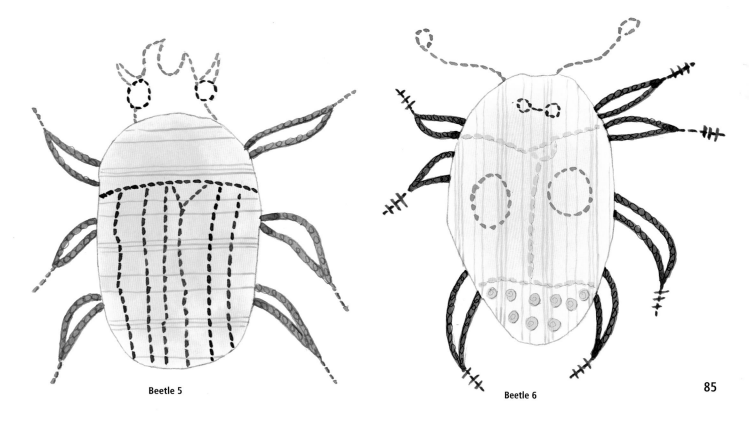

Beetle 5

Beetle 6

	Stitch	Color
Beetle 7		
Back lines and eyes	Backstitch	Bronze
Back circles	Backstitch	Airforce blue
Antennae	Backstitch	Charcoal
Legs	Chain stitch	Pale aqua
Feet	Small straight stitches	Pale aqua
Beetle 8		
Back pattern	Chain stitch	Pale yellow
Legs	Chain stitch	Pale olive
Feet	Small straight stitches	Pale olive
Eyes and antennae	Backstitch and small straight stitches	Pale aqua
Beetle 9		
Back lines	Backstitch	Pale yellow
Eyes	Backstitch	Pale aqua
Legs	Chain stitch	Pale aqua
Feet	Backstitch and small straight stitches	Pale aqua
Antennae	Backstitch	Very dark green
Beetle 10		
Back lines and eyes	Backstitch	Bronze
Dots on back	French knots	Airforce blue
Legs	Chain stitch	Bronze
Feet	Small straight stitches	Bronze
Antennae	Small straight stitches over backstitch	Airforce blue
Beetle 11		
Back lines	Backstitch	Pale aqua
Eyes	Backstitch	Charcoal
Dots on back	French knots	Pale olive
Legs	Chain stitch	Charcoal
Feet	Small straight stitches over backstitch	Charcoal
Antennae	Backstitch	Pale olive
Beetle 12		
Back lines	Backstitch	Pale olive
Head	Backstitch	Airforce blue
Legs	Chain stitch	Airforce blue
Feet	Small straight stitches	Airforce blue
Antennae	Backstitch and double cross stitch	Bronze

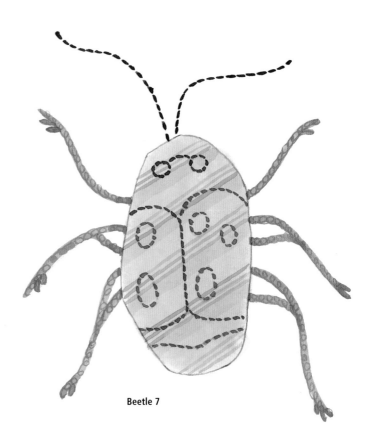

Beetle 7

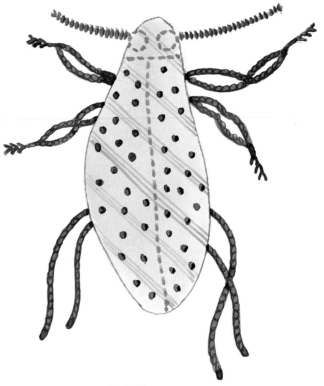

Beetle 10

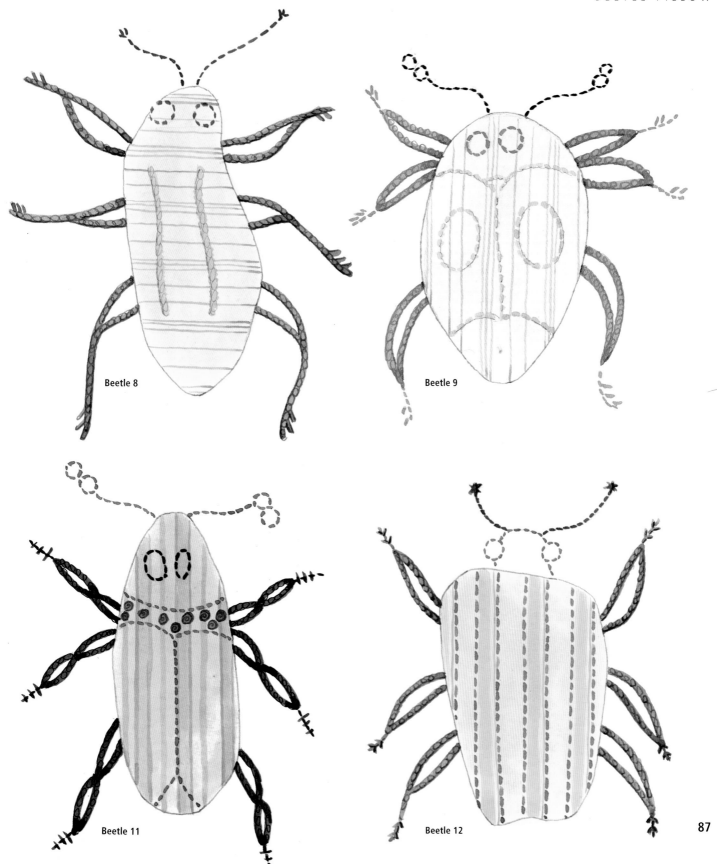

Beetle 8

Beetle 9

Beetle 11

Beetle 12

embroidered buttons

Buttons are like little jewels in the embroiderer's workbasket, and are frequently undervalued. These "notions," which serve to keep one side of our clothes in touch with the other, usually last much longer than the garment they originally adorned and deserve more respect than they get. A handmade button is truly a treasure, and a little embroidery can transform a simple button into a piece of workaday art. Embroidered buttons can be personalized with monograms, flowers, or a design that reflects the fabric used. A selection of miniature motifs and an alphabet are given on pages 106–107.

Flower buttons

Stitches used
satin stitch (page 50),
stem stitch (page 25),
French knots (page 76),
backstitch (page 24).

Here, buttons have been elevated to purely decorative rather than functional objects. The tiny flowers on the buttoned pillow reflect the coloring but contrast strongly with the geometric check pattern of the pillow fabric.

		Anchor	DMC
■	Bright pink	41	961
■	Purply pink	1019	3722
■	Pale green	854	3013
■	Lime green	279	734
■	Mid green	268	469

Quantity
One 9yd/8m skein of each color.
NB Use one strand of thread throughout.

You will need
Fabric for each button, large enough to stretch in an embroidery hoop frame (keeping the fabric taut is important in achieving detail in this miniature embroidery)
Button-covering kit(s), large enough for the embroidery – those illustrated are 1¼" (3cm) (flowers) and 1⅜" (3.5cm) (initials) approx in diameter (some fabric stores run a button-covering service)

Embroidery hoop frame
Crewel (embroidery) needle size 9 or 10
Anchor or DMC cotton floss in the colors shown below left

To work the embroidery
1 Trace and transfer the pattern onto the fabric, using method 1 described on page 16.
2 Fill the petals with bright pink satin stitch, up to the center circle.
3 Outline the petals with backstitch in purply pink.
4 Fill the flower centers with French knots in lime green.
5 Fill the leaf with pale green satin stitch, using mid green to mark the veins.
6 Stitch the stem and outline the leaf with mid green stem stitch.

To finish
Finish the buttons according to the instructions supplied with the button-covering kit.

Monogrammed buttons

Stitches used
satin stitch (page 50),
backstitch (page 24).

The monogrammed buttons on this pillowcase lend it a chic, tailored look that could co-ordinate with other furnishings in the bedroom.

You will need
Fabric, needle, hoop, and button-covering kit as for Flower Buttons
Cotton floss in a color of your choice (the buttons illustrated use Anchor 1019/DMC 315)

To work the embroidery
1 Select a letter from the patterns on

pages 106–107 and reduce to the required size on a photocopier.
2 Trace and transfer the pattern onto the fabric using method 1, as described on page 16.
3 Use satin stitch, worked at a slight angle to accentuate the curves, for all but the very thin lines, which are worked in tiny backstitches.

crazy patchwork

Crazy patchwork – sometimes erroneously called crazy quilting (which is only created when the top is stitched to a padded backing) – originated in America in the latter part of the nineteenth century. Unlike ordinary patchwork, it was not the product of necessity, but a fashion that resulted in kits and patterns being produced to satisfy the market.

Typically, these patchworks are made of scraps of silk and velvet arranged randomly like crazy paving and appliquéd onto a cotton backing, or onto cotton squares that are then stitched together. However, the one illustrated has been carefully planned, and benefits from the balanced patterning and clever use of the various fabrics and colors. At first glance it appears random, but gradually the quirky symmetry of the design emerges. Though the fabrics may be different in the pattern repeats, the color families are usually the same.

The many seams of crazy patchwork are typically sewn over with fancy stitches. Monograms, dates, and other personal motifs are often included too, making these pieces ideal vehicles for commemorating special occasions. A wedding patchwork, for example, can be made using scraps from the dress, and even a piece from the groom's tie, stitched with silk in the colors of the bouquet and including mementos of the day in the surface embroidery. The fabrics used for the crazy patchwork shown here include silks from ties, lightweight velvets, ribbons, and furnishing taffetas and silks of similar weights. You can use any fabrics as long as the weights are roughly matched. If they are too different, the patchwork will not look harmonious.

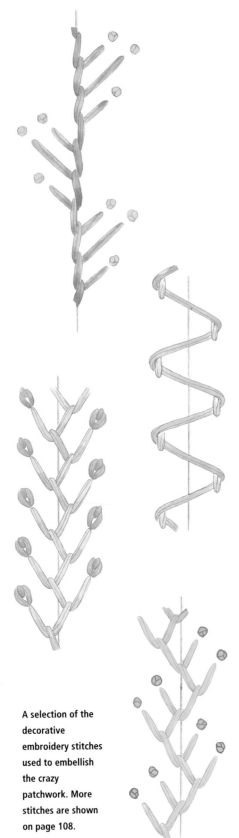

A selection of the decorative embroidery stitches used to embellish the crazy patchwork. More stitches are shown on page 108.

You will need

For the quilt:

Enough medium-weight cotton to cut 25 pieces, each 10½" (27cm) square

51" (130cm) square backing fabric

Assorted fabric scraps to cover all cotton fabric squares

1yd (1m) black moiré, 36" (90cm) wide, for binding

Matching sewing thread

For the embroidery:

Crewel (embroidery) needle

Anchor or DMC pearl cotton in selection of colors and weights

To make the patchwork

1 Cut the fabric into 25 pieces 10½" (27cm) square. Cut the fabric scraps into the types of shape shown on page 109.

2 Mark the center of each cotton square (see page 16) and draw a 9½" (24cm) square centrally on each one.

3 Arrange the fabric shapes into patterns fitting into the marked squares. To make a planned (as opposed to random) quilt, like the one shown, you will need to repeat some of the patterns and arrange them in a regular order, similar to the layout shown on page 108. In this patchwork, the corner templates have a heart motif, which is a shape sympathetic to a corner and immediately recognizable. Four rising sun shapes are used farther in, angled to fan outward, hinting at a circle. The center square contains a monogram and date. Similar colors are used for the pattern repeats, which help the eye to identify the symmetry.

4 Turn under the raw edges of the fabric shapes and baste to the cotton squares. Slip stitch the fabric shapes to secure them and remove the basting. Press.

To join and embroider

1 Arrange the individual squares in rows of five and machine stitch them together with a ½" (1.5cm) seam allowance. Press the seams open. Then stitch the five rows together and press the seams open.

2 Embroider over abutting edges with linear stitches in colors of your choice, adding any other stitch that enhances the effect. On this quilt, the seams between the squares are covered with running stitch laced with two strands of pearl cotton in various colors. The stitches are worked not only over the seams and the joins of the appliqué, but also to decorate the fabrics themselves and to accentuate their own patterning. Where ribbon has been used as a patch, the stitching is almost a caricature of its own pattern, for little French knots point up a picot edge, and a line of bold gold stars are awarded to a military-style striped ribbon. Elsewhere, the stitches have been adapted to fit the various shapes. Graduated buttonhole and chevron stitches can accommodate curves, straight stitch is used in a number of inventive ways, herringbone stitch and feather stitch feature strongly, and no seam is left unadorned.

3 Back the patchwork by laying it out on the backing fabric and basting down around each square. Machine stitch around the outer edge with raw edges showing. Remove basting threads. Trim the backing fabric to match the front.

To bind the edges

1 Cut and join the black moiré fabric into strips long enough to bind each edge, adding a hem at each end of two of the strips. The strips should be double the required width of the finished binding, plus ⅝" (1.5cm) seam allowances.

2 Lay the shorter strips along opposite edges of the patchwork, right sides together, and stitch to the patchwork with a ⅝" (1.5cm) seam allowance.

3 Press the strips and fold them over the raw edges. Press again. Hem the strips to the back of the patchwork by hand, just inside the machine-stitched line, in the same way as for bias binding.

4 Turn under the short ends of the other two strips and press. Bind the remaining two sides of the patchwork as before.

cross stitch
& lazy daisy
border

This sophisticated border pattern, shown here on a tablecloth, is unusual in its use of cross stitch as a background, framing the pretty lazy daisy stitch flowers in a ribbon formation. The cross stitch is a double version, with a straight cross sewn on top of the usual diagonally formed cross stitch. The base crosses are all the same color, while the top crosses are stitched in two different colors in zigzag lines, adding an unexpected dimension to an otherwise formal pattern.

Unlike most cross stitch patterns, the stitches here are all made separately, with a thread or two of fabric dividing one from the next – the stitcher has not counted the linen weave over which the crosses are made, but has worked the pattern entirely by eye. The effect is less rigid than some cross stitch designs, and makes a refreshing change from "counted thread" work. The use of lazy daisy stitch for the flowers is straightforward but the coloring is subtle, with two shades of one color being used in each vignette – the artistry has to be admired.

The pattern can be used to edge a wide variety of items including the tablecloth for which instructions are given here, napkins, guest towels, and pillows.

Stitches used
double cross stitch (page 52),
lazy daisy stitch (page 75),
stem stitch (page 25),
French knots (page 76),
drawn thread work (page 38).

You will need
32" (80cm) square fine evenweave linen
Crewel (embroidery) needle size 8
Anchor or DMC cotton floss in the colors shown on page 96

To work the embroidery
1 Plan out the pattern on the fabric as described on page 16. The finished tablecloth measures 25" (63cm) square, the embroidery 21" (53cm) square (outside measurement). The pattern given on page 96 shows one corner of the design and several repeats of the border pattern. Trace the parts of the design required and transfer to the fabric, using method 3 described on pages 16–17. Draw in all the cross stitches unless you are confident that you can place them successfully by eye.

2 There is no particular order of stitching the border, although it is easier to achieve even stitches if the green squares have already been stitched. The lazy daisy flowers should be worked before putting the French knots in their centers, as the knots will overlap the stitches in places. Start at the point of each shape to be filled with cross stitch. This will make it easier to keep the crosses in even rows.

To finish
Turn under a ¾" (2cm) hem, with a drawn thread border if you wish. Alternatively, work a plain hem, mitering the corners as follows. Press a crease at the outer edge of the hem. Fold in the corners and trim to ¼" (5mm) (fig 1). Fold under ¼" (5mm) all around (fig 2), then turn under the rest of the hem (fig 3).

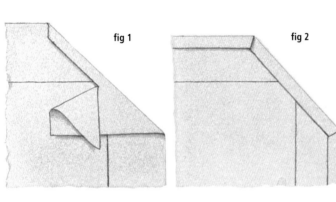

fig 1

fig 2

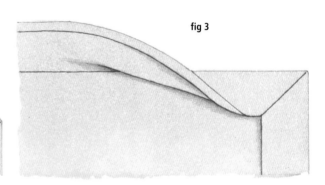

fig 3

NB Use three strands of Anchor or DMC cotton floss throughout, except for the top crosses of the cross stitch, for which only two strands are used.

Flowers:	Anchor	DMC	Quantity
Bright yellow	302	742	1
Cream	300	7451	1
Dark blue	123	7911	1
Mid blue	143	7981	1
Dark purple	102	5501	1
Bright purple	110	37461	1
Dark pink	88	7181	1
Pale pink	85	36091	1

	Anchor	DMC	Quantity
Leaves and flower centers:			
Pale yellow	293	727	3
Stem stitch outline:			
Mid green	210	911	2
Cross stitch filling:			
Pale brown	677	8410	4
Orange	330	946	2
Light green	209	912	2

This pattern shows one corner of the design and several repeats of the border pattern. Trace the parts as required and transfer onto the fabric.

Patterns & motifs

On the following pages you will find a wealth of extra motifs and stitches to extend the scope of the projects in the book even further. There are alternative designs for shells, appliqué creatures, and cutwork flowers as well as a complete set of letters and numerals for monograms and dates. Extra floral motifs of all sizes are also provided, so that you can find ideas for decorating a whole range of items from buttons to bedspreads. In addition, creative stitch variations for embellishing crazy patchwork are given along with a suggested layout for a more structured type of crazy quilt.

cutwork flowers

See Cutwork Leaves on page 40

This floral cutwork pattern is a repeating one, so it may be continued in any direction as required. It can form a border along the edge of a curtain or tablecloth in the same way as the leaf design on page 40, or it can be built up into an overall pattern for the center of a pillow cover or a table mat.

The outlines of the petals and leaves are shown with a heavy line and buttonhole bars are also indicated. The areas where the fabric is to be cut away are differentiated with shading. When you are working buttonhole stitch around the edges of the motifs, make sure that the looped part of the stitching faces the areas to be cut away as this prevents the fabric from unraveling. Further details of flower centers, shading, and leaf patterning may be added as required.

blue-and-white motifs

See Blue-and-white Bedspread
on page 54

These simple motifs offer an alternative to the patterns shown on the blue-and-white bedspread project on pages 54–59 and are inspired by the designs in the collection of American Colonial embroidery gathered by the Deerfield Society of Blue and White Needlework, in Massachusetts. Typically, these patterns consist of flowing stalks from which flowers and fruit grow. The embroideries themselves were usually executed in hand-dyed threads in shades of blues.

This placement diagram indicates where each motif should be positioned on the bedspread. Some of the motifs have been reversed to give more variation. Enlarge the motifs to 164% on a photocopier before transferring to the fabric.

repeating shell patterns

See Shell Pillows on page 78

Simple shapes repeated in rows or around a circle can make effective, all-over patterning. The cockleshell pattern opposite (used for the blue shell pillow on page 79) is made from just one shape, turned in two directions and alternately decorated, which leads the eye to see diagonal rows of motifs even though the pattern is created from straight ones.

Although this shell arrangement was designed to be embroidered in French knots, outline stitches would be a good alternative, and more fancy filling stitches could be used to embellish the shells further.

Other shell shapes are also illustrated here as alternatives to the cockleshell. Make several photocopies or tracings, cut them out, and arrange them until you have a pattern you like. Trace again and make several copies. Lay them out to fill the size and shape of the item you wish to embroider.

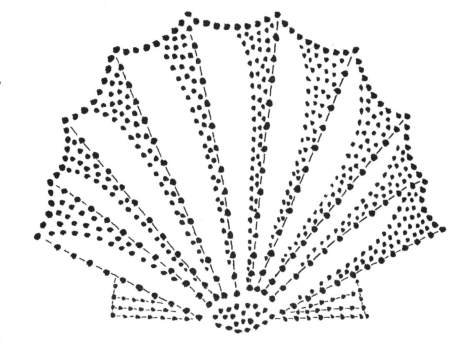

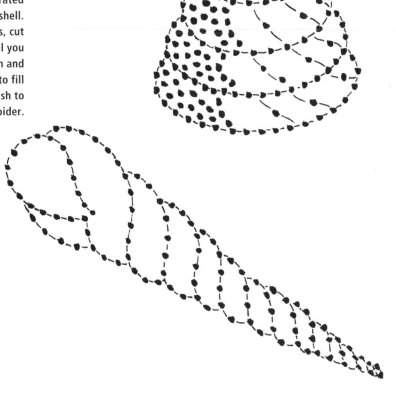

appliqué creatures

See Beetle Pillow on page 82

Butterflies or snails, birds or caterpillars – all are good alternatives to the appliqué creatures on the Beetle Pillow illustrated on page 83 and can be arranged in rows to give a similar effect. For the stitching, much depends on your choice of fabric. Nevertheless, all the motifs give you the opportunity to develop your own stitch ideas and colors. The markings are suggestions for patterning, which can easily be changed to suit the fabrics and stitches you wish to use.

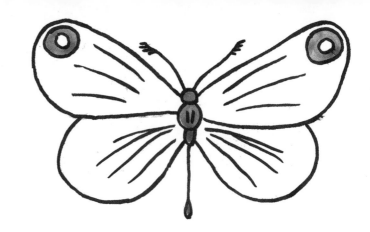

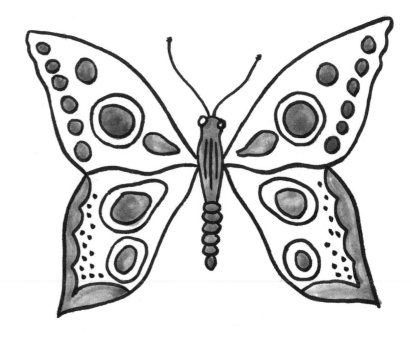

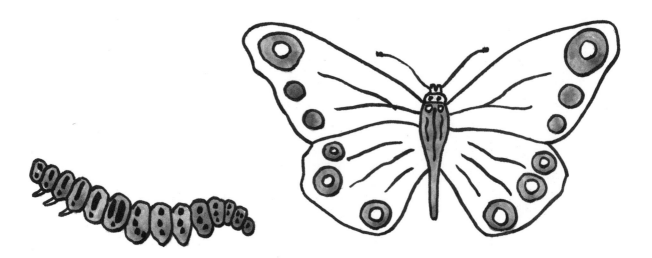

miniature motifs

See Embroidered Buttons on page 88

Choose the initials, or numbers, you need for buttons or household linen. Embroider them in satin stitch except for the thin lines which can be worked with very small backstitches.

The tiny floral motifs provide some alternatives for delicate embellishments. Use just one strand of embroidery floss for this fine work. The larger motifs will provide inspiration for embroidery on all kinds of items, including table linen, free-form samplers and potpourri sachets.

crazy patchwork

See Crazy Patchwork on page 90

Decorating crazy patchwork is a wonderful opportunity to combine every stitch you can think of with another one. The stitches can be laced together with contrasting threads and colors to cover joins and seams or to embellish the patterns existing in the fabric. It is fun to create combinations that lend themselves to the decoration of a straight line or a curve - placed with care, the angles of the stitches add a further interesting dimension to the design.

The crazy patchwork panels opposite are similar to those on the quilt illustrated on page 90. Some have recognizable motifs, others are irregular; use some of these shapes as a guide when cutting your own patches if you wish.

The diagram below shows the layout for the quilt on page 90, in which panels A and B are repeated in a regular order. For a completely random quilt, you do not need to join the panels in any particular order, but try to keep a good balance of colour and tone overall.

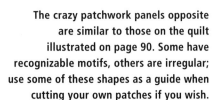

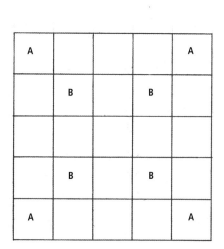

index

acknowledgements

The author would like to thank the following: Ciba Vaughan, a great friend who lives in Boston, without whom I would have found it difficult even to start writing a book on embroidery. Her advice, enthusiasm and huge fund of knowledge were invaluable, and the fax lines across the Atlantic buzzed with our "embroidery exchange". Many of the pieces illustrated here come from her collection, and she made the Crazy patchwork specially for this book.

Karen Spurgin also needs a special thank you for her refreshing and modern designs: the Beetle Pillow, the Embroidered Buttons and the Cutwork Curtain.

Cara Ackerman at DMC and Julie Gill at J & P Coats were enormously helpful in providing fabrics and threads, always at short notice. Jenny Fitzgerald Bond gave me valuable technical advice which was most useful. The series editor, Jane O'Shea, was wonderfully patient throughout and always found a way to solve problems. I am most grateful to her.

Publisher's acknowledgements

The publishers would like to thank the following for lending fabrics, threads and other items for inclusion in the photography: Jane Bell, The Chelsea Design Company, Coats Crafts UK, Designer's Guild, DMC, The Gallery of Antique Costume and Textiles, Cath Kidston, John Lewis, V V Rouleaux.

We would also like to thank Gabi Tubbs for her inspired styling of the photographs and Pia Tryde for a superb location and her hospitality.